THE NEW CHARLESTON CHEF'S TABLE

EXTRAORDINARY RECIPES FROM THE HEART OF THE OLD SOUTH

HOLLY HERRICK

Globe Pequot

Guilford, Connecticut

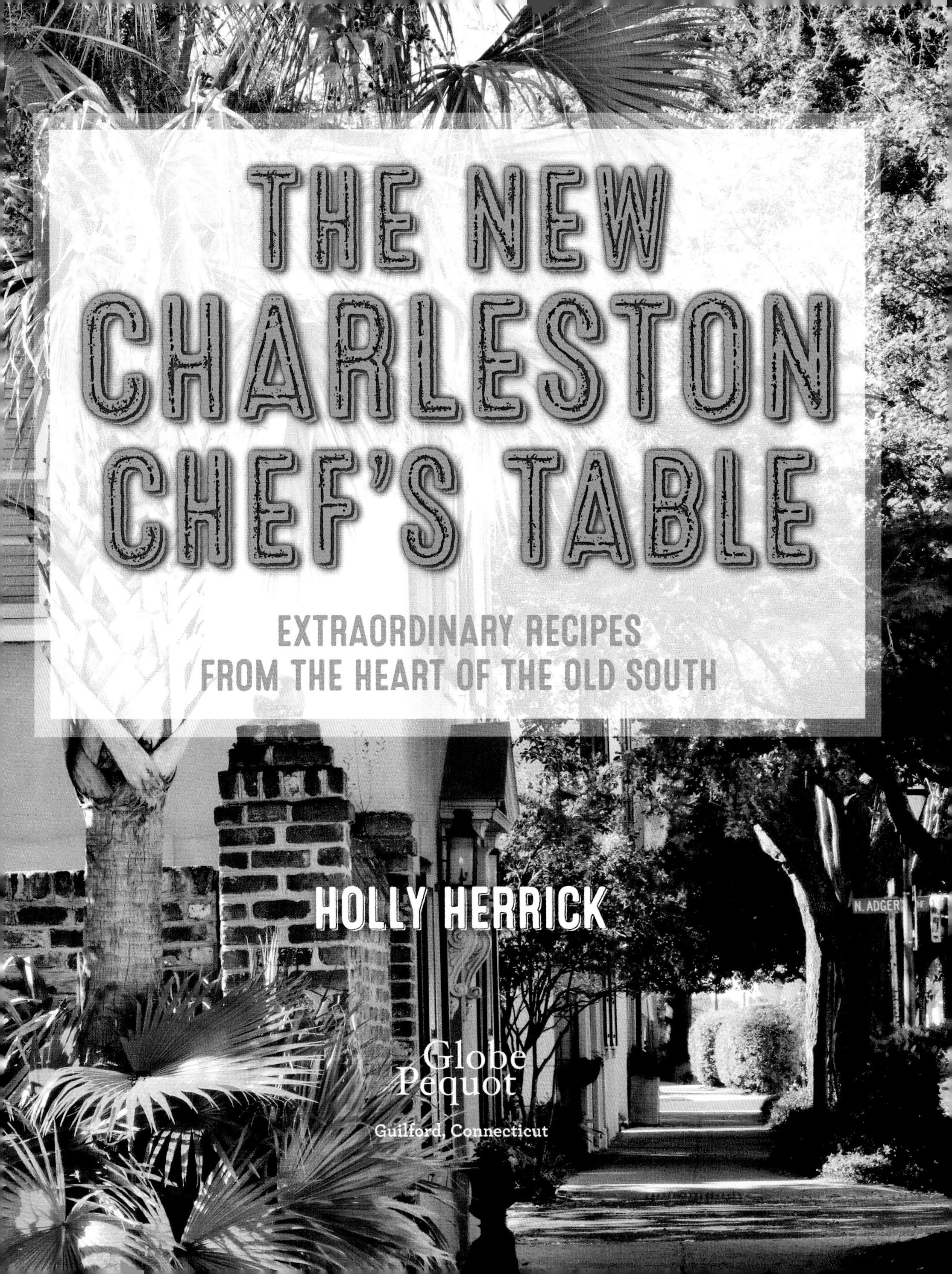

To Michael. Thank you for always being there.

And, for my darling Rocky Rocken puppy for always making me laugh and filling my heart with love, daily.

And, to beautiful Charleston and her talented chefs and food and beverage professionals for providing a constant stream of deliciousness and inspiration. And, for making yourselves and your recipes available to help me write this book.

Globe Pequot

An imprint of The Rowman & Littlefield Publishing Group, Inc.
4501 Forbes Blvd., Ste. 200
Lanham, MD 20706
www.rowman.com

Distributed by NATIONAL BOOK NETWORK

British Library Cataloguing in Publication Information Available

Library of Congress Cataloging-in-Publication Data Available

ISBN 978-1-4930-2933-4 (hardcover)
ISBN 978-1-4930-2934-1 (e-book)

∞™ The paper used in this publication meets the minimum requirements of American National Standard for Information Sciences—Permanence of Paper for Printed Library Materials, ANSI/NISO Z39.48-1992.

Printed in the United States of America

CONTENTS

Acknowledgments

After nearly two decades of living and working in Charleston as a restaurant critic and food writer, I haven't been able to decide if the food here tastes so good because Charleston is just so darn beautiful or if it's because Charleston's beauty attracts so many wonderful chefs. Isn't beauty drawn to beauty? Is it cause or effect? Thankfully, these questions don't really demand answers. Instead, we're all invited to sit back and reap the gorgeous gustatory rewards.

And so I extend a huge and hearty thank-you to Charleston and to all of the city's dedicated and talented chefs who give of themselves daily to produce artistry in their kitchens. Without their generosity and their time, this book would not have been possible. Thank you all for answering my questions and providing tested recipes for some of your most celebrated dishes. It's been truly fun getting to know all of you better.

Also, special thanks to my editor at Globe Pequot Press, Amy Lyons (and for the original edition, Heather Carreiro) and to my agent Joelle Delbourgo. All believed in this book enough and stood by me for the long journey to make it a reality in its original form and in this, the updated second edition.

Thank you to all my friends, family, and neighbors who listened to me talking about this for as long as I did and for walking me through occasional bouts of deadline panic.

Finally, my canine angel, Tann Mann, thank you for just being sweet, chocolate you. And, to Mr. Purrfect, my amazing, dog-like cat who was by my side at my desk and in my kitchen for nearly all the writing of this, the second edition, and newly named *The New Charleston Chef's Table*.

Photo credits: p. i MarynaG/Shutterstock.com; p. iii, vi, viii Christopher Shane Brown; p. x–1 KeithBrileyPhotography/Shutterstock.com; p. 3 Christopher Shane Brown; p. 5 Christopher Shane Brown; p. 7 Christopher Shane Brown; p. 10 Christopher Shane Brown; p. 12, 13 Courtesy of Charleston Grill; p. 15 9to9studio/Shutterstock.com; p. 16 Matthew Orselli/Shutterstock.com; p. 20 Christopher Shane Brown; p. 21 iStock.com/Shaiith; p. 23 Christopher Shane Brown; p. 24 Sarah Nielson; p. 28 Courtesy of Rita's Seaside Grille; p. 31 John Smoak; p. 33 iStock.com/Creative-Family; p. 36–37 p. 7 Christopher Shane Brown; p. 39 Olivia Rae James; p. 42 Courtesy of Cru Café on Pinckney Street; p. 44, 45 Courtesy of The Glass Onion; p. 46 and p. 48 Ben Reitz; p. 47 Peter Frank Edwards; p. 49 Bob Waggoner; p. 50 Dominique Chantepie; p. 52–53 iStockphoto.com/NorthHatley; p. 54 iStock.com/NoDerog; p. 61 Courtesy of Middleton Place Foundation; p. 62 Courtesy of 39 Rue de Jean; p. 63 Christopher Shane Brown; p. 66 iStock.com/sallyjshintaffer; p. 67 Christopher Shane Brown; p. 69 Andrew Cebulka; p. 72–73 Christopher Shane Brown; p. 75 Christopher Shane Brown; p. 76 Schanen Smith/High Vibe Media; p. 77 iStock.com/Yulia-Images; p. 79 iStock.com/joannawnuk; p. 80 Courtesy of Five Loaves Café; p. 84, 85 Courtesy of Gaulart & Maliclet; p. 86 iStock.com/mattgrandbois; p. 88 Courtesy of Boxcar Betty's; p. 90, 92 Courtesy of Butcher & Bee; p. 94 Courtesy of Minero; p. 96 iStock.com/karinsasaki; p. 98, 99, 100 Courtesy of Edmund's Oast; p. 102–103 iStock.com/SeanPavonePhoto; p. 105, 106 Christopher Shane Brown; p. 109 Christopher Shane Brown; p. 114, 116 Andrew Thomas Lee; p. 117 Courtesy of The Grocery; p. 118, 120 Andrew Cebulka; p. 122, 123 Chrys Rynearson; p. 124–125 Serge Skiba/Shutterstock.com; p. 126 Courtesy of Bowen's Island Restaurant; p. 128, 129 Courtesy of Hank's; p. 130 Christopher Shane Brown; p. 137 Courtesy of Anson Restaurant; p. 138 iStock.com/bhofack2; p. 140 Molly Joseph Photography; p. 141 Courtesy of Toast of Charleston; p. 143, 145 Courtesy of The Ordinary; p. 146, 148 Courtesy of Zero Restaurant + Bar; p. 151 Olivia Rae James; p. 153 Courtesy of High Thyme; p. 155, 156 Courtesy of Coda del Pesce; p. 158 Courtesy of 167 Raw; p. 159 Cassandra Michelle; p. 160–161 Dave Allen Photography/Shutterstock.com; p. 162, 163 Andrew Cebulka; p. 164 jwkpec.com; p. 168 Christopher Shane Brown; p. 171 Christopher Shane Brown; p. 173, 174 Courtesy of Louis Barbecue; p. 175, 176 Andrew Cebulka; p. 179, 180 Courtesy of Halls Chophouse; p. 181 Susan Lucas; p. 182–183 Cvandyke/Shutterstock.com; p. 184, 186 Courtesy of Hominy Grill; p. 185 Christopher Shane Brown; p. 188 Christopher Shane Brown; p. 193, 194, 195 Courtesy of Mex 1 Coastal Cantina; p. 196 Courtesy of Cannon Green; p. 199 Courtesy of The Macintosh; p. 202 Courtesy of Brown's Court Bakery; p. 203 and 204 Courtesy of goat.sheep.cow; p. 205 Courtesy of Callie's Hot Little Biscuit; p. 208–209 James Kirkikis/Shutterstock.com; p. 211 Courtesy of 181 Palmer; p. 214 iStock.com/awdebenham; p. 218 iStock.com/neiljlangan; p. 222 Helene Dujardin

Preface

Much has changed in the world and in Charleston since the first edition of *Charleston Chef's Table* was written, largely during 2008 and published in December, 2009.

Then, the world was in a state of fiscal uncertainty and the United States was in the throes of what would eventually be called The Great Recession. Still, as stalwart, brave Charleston has done so many times in the past during times of strife, famine, war, and natural disasters, Charleston muddled through. In fact, not only muddled through, but roared through that time and the subsequent years until now, morphing from a relatively blushing teenager culinary star, into an international and national culinary destination of the highest order.

Then, Charleston was already a magnificent culinary destination. But since, James Beard nominations and culinary accolades from virtually every medium possible are commonplace. *Conde Nast Traveler* Readers' Choice Award 2016 named Charleston the best small city destination in the United States. Chefs Sean Brock and Mike Lata are known and lauded nationally and internationally.

With that kind of recognition, there has been huge growth. Restaurants that demand regular visits have popped up all over town and suburbs in greater Charleston. Where formal downtown destinations with white linen tablecloths and high price tags were once the order of the day, casual, increasingly eclectic, farm-to-table driven eateries are spreading uptown well beyond the perceived restaurant "border" that was once King Street and Line Street with the likes of Leon's Oyster Shop (page 46) way uptown and Chez Nous (page 150) situated on the once unthinkable edge of The Crosstown highway.

This level of change and increased heights of culinary bars across all restaurant spectrums, of course lead to the demise of restaurants that didn't meet current standards, and the increase of many new that do. In this edition, I've bid farewell to over half of the restaurants featured in the original version due to closings or quality slippage, and added over sixty more. Thus, in many ways, this is almost an entirely new edition.

Still, with all of the change and growth, much of what I and so much of the world loves about Charleston has remained the same. The waters that surround her still afford some of the most buttery, sweet shrimp in the world, and slurp-inducing, briny oysters. The colonial and antebellum skyline remains dotted with the steeples of 200 churches sketched against blazing, orange-pink sunsets. And the marshes, verdant green in the summer and turning to a beige gold by autumn, still sway with sea breezes rippling the harbor and flirting with the light of the sun.

INTRODUCTION

As American author, poet, and Charleston native DuBose Heyward wrote in "Dusk," a poem to Charleston, she is indeed "alone among the cities." Her haunting colonial and antebellum architectural curves and the luscious winding waterways that embrace her would be enough for Charleston to claim a unique beauty and presence. But there is much more. A big part of Charleston's radiance is her delicious status as one of this country's most popular dining and tourist destinations.

To understand the general and culinary present, we have to look briefly to the past. Unlike the other American colonies, Charleston, founded in 1670, was chartered by fun-loving, party-hearty King Charles II of England, and before long the young town embraced religious tolerance for its residents. Immigrants from England were looking for a chance to prosper and have a good time like the wealthy landowners of Merry England, while many immigrants from France, Ireland, Scotland, and elsewhere came to escape religious persecution. Thus, unlike Quaker Philadelphia and Puritan Boston, Charleston, also known as "The Holy City," was home to a cultural and culinary mix, one that was infinitely larger (it had, for example, the biggest French population of any colony), more complex, and arguably more sophisticated than her colonial contemporaries.

But it was the Lowcountry—a sixty-mile stretch of low-lying land that includes Charleston—whose geography, marshes, and tidal-driven interchanges of fresh and salt water led to the city's largest and most tragic immigration. Slaves, mostly from the rice-producing region of Sierra Leone in Africa, came to the port city by the thousands to help planters grow and harvest rice crops that quickly made Charleston one of the country's wealthiest cities, a status she held until the Civil War. Like the French, Jews, and Scottish Baptists, the Africans brought with them a taste for the flavors and ingredients of their homelands, including okra, rice, and field peas. Unlike slaves in other colonies, slaves in this area worked on a task system. They were allowed and encouraged to work their private gardens and do their own cooking, according to historian Robert Stockton. In this way, the slaves preserved their culinary traditions, traditions that would later trickle down into Charleston's famous dishes like gumbo and hoppin' John.

In this solitary melting pot of wealth and sophistication, a cornucopia of seafood and produce ingredients and an early-established insatiability for good food and good times endure to this day. In Charleston, one does not get "drunk" or "hung over" but instead "over served." But what and where Charlestonians and visitors eat have changed since days past—especially in the last twenty-five years.

Long saddled with episodes of poverty, devastating hurricanes, earthquakes, and fires (especially after the Civil War), Charlestonians developed a driving sense of survival, pride, and practicality. These qualities led them to preserve many of the historic structures—and the endearing Southern charm—that would eventually bring the tourists, the money, and the vast pool of delicious restaurants Charleston now enjoys.

Charleston's culinary and cultural evolution came in three distinct waves. Long-time resident and author Barbara Hagerty describes Charleston between World War II and the late-1970s as "backwater" or "provincial," offering only two restaurants of note. The first wave of change began in 1977, when Gian Carlo Menotti chose Charleston as the site of what would become a wildly successful annual art and cultural festival, Spoleto USA. At about the same time, newly elected Charleston mayor Joseph P. Riley undertook extensive and successful efforts to rejuvenate the dilapidated downtown shopping area, creating the Charleston Place shopping center and a luxury hotel. Both proved to be magnets for tourists, and the new culinary and hospitality school Johnson & Wales (now located in Charlotte, North Carolina) would train chefs like Peninsula Grill's Robert Carter to feed the rapidly evolving gustatory appetites of tourists and locals alike.

The next wave of change came in the aftermath of a tragedy, Hurricane Hugo, on September 21, 1989. "Relief poured in from around the nation and the world, both in volunteers and funds. Insurance companies, some of which went out of business because of Hugo, paid over $3.2 billion in claims," writes local historian, Robert Rosen, in his book *A Short History of Charleston* (University of South Carolina Press, 1997). In the storm's aftermath, groundbreaking Southern chefs like Magnolia's Donald Barickman and Slightly North of Broad's Frank Lee seized the opportunity to show the world the wonders of grits prepared with cream and the sultriness of real she-crab soup. South Carolina native Frank Lee even introduced something relatively exotic to Charleston at the time—pad thai. Charleston experienced an artistic renaissance with Hollywood coming to town to film famous movies like *North and South* and *The Prince of Tides* and the literary works of Pat Conroy, Dottie Frank, and Alexandra Ripley. And a fat money trail of the super-rich leading to downtown and the resort islands of Kiawah, Seabrook, and Wild Dunes, followed.

Eventually, new chefs like McCrady's Sean Brock brought sophisticated innovation through sous vide technique, spinning it with the homespun goodness of vegetables he raises in his own garden. Hominy Grill's Robert Stehling was named Southeast Chef of the Year in 2008, FIG's Mike Lata was named Southeast Chef of the Year in 2009, and many more, from Bob Waggoner to Lauren Mitterer, have received James Beard nominations. Charleston's annual Food & Wine Festival (founded in 2006) is another testimony to how utterly edible Charleston has become.

This book was written to celebrate beautiful Charleston and her extraordinarily talented chefs from restaurants small and large, simple and fancy. Restaurants were chosen for inclusion based first and foremost on the high quality of the food they consistently deliver but also for their unique personalities. Feel free to make the recipes just as the chefs do or modify them and make them your own. One caveat: Always taste and season carefully as you work. It's essential to good cooking.

All of the restaurants featured in *The New Charleston Chef's Table* are located within a thirty-mile radius of the downtown peninsula. Most are located on or near the peninsula or in nearby suburbs like West Ashley and Mount Pleasant. This book is intended to be as much a recipe book for cooking enthusiasts as an ode to Charleston for those who love her from afar, for those who have been lucky enough to visit, and perhaps for the luckiest of all—those who call Charleston home. Please think of these recipes as a gracious invitation, extended directly to you, to visit and taste beautiful Charleston, literally and figuratively. For that is the intention behind the words on the pages that follow.

We nod to greet some friends we meet
As through wrought iron gate
We slowly pass bright polished brass,
And hope that we are late.
Like honey bees in acacia trees
Distant voices hum,
And from within, a merry din,
As nearer the house we come
People stand like steeples,
High-ball ice-chimes in hand,
Like buoy bells the tinkling swells
Across the social strand.

"Seaside Similes" by S. Lewis Johnson,
Sparks from My Chimney, copyright © 1963.
Reprinted by permission of the author's daughter,
Kathleen Johnson Hall.

starters

Since the city's earliest days, Charlestonians have reveled in the pleasures of petite bites paired with libations. While back then it was often port or Madeira with cheese sticks or benne wafers, these days the choices are considerably vaster and decidedly more international. And, because Charleston is literally surrounded by water—both salt water and brackish—it's a ripe breeding ground for glorious seafood that often starts off many a feast. Especially the shrimp, oysters, and crab for which The Lowcountry is so celebrated that happen to pair beautifully with classic festive occasion Champagne.

Not surprisingly, in this chapter these briny jewels are prominently featured in several new recipes, including Charleston Grill's remarkably simple and sweetly delicious lump blue crab cakes with creek shrimp and a zesty lime tomato vinaigrette, Peninsula Grill's Lady's Island Oysters Casino, and Rita's Seaside Grill's creamy and comforting warm blue crab dip. Landlubbers will revel in Monza's beefy ricotta meatballs in sausage and pepper marinara sauce, Little Jack's Tavern's old school, creamy and pungent beef tartare, and Red Orchids Bistro's sweet barbecue buns washed down with a glass of sake.

JESTINE'S KITCHEN

251 Meeting Street, downtown
(843) 722-7224
jestineskitchen.com
Owner: Dana Berlin Strange

Opened in part as a communal legacy for owner Dana Berlin Strange's childhood nanny, Jestine Matthews, Jestine's Kitchen steadily cranks out the kind of food that Dana and three generations of her family enjoyed under Jestine's loving care. Though Jestine passed at the ripe old age of 112 more than two decades ago, her spirit and hospitality truly do live on at Jestine's.

Dana reserves a few seats in the back for regulars, but the space teems with those who have come from near and far to savor Jestine's towering plate of fried chicken and top it off with airy coconut cream pie—the real custard, real whipped cream, and house-made pastry variety—washed down with sweet tea or Jestine's "table wine."

Instead of bread, every meal at Jestine's begins with a petite diner-style bowl of cool, refreshing Refrigerator Pickles. "My mom and grandmother made them regularly when we were growing up," says Dana. After a night in the fridge, fresh "garden variety" cucumbers are transformed into crisp slivers of Southern goodness. Eat them up quickly, however, because they get too soft after three or four days, according to Dana.

REFRIGERATOR PICKLES

(MAKES 1 QUART OR APPROXIMATELY 8 APPETIZER PORTIONS)

2 medium cucumbers, cut in half lengthwise and thinly sliced

1 onion, halved and thinly sliced

2 tablespoons whole black peppercorns

¼ cup white wine vinegar

¼ cup granulated sugar

Pinch of salt

Special equipment: 1 quart-size glass Mason (or another brand) jar

In a medium bowl, toss together the cucumbers, onion, and peppercorns. Pack them loosely in the quart-size jar. Combine the vinegar, sugar, and salt in a separate small bowl, whisking to combine. Pour the vinegar mixture into the jar, covering the cucumbers and onion. (Note: You may have a little more or less vinegar mixture than you need depending on the size of the cucumbers. The ratio of vinegar to sugar is always the same—50/50—so whip up more if you need it.) Seal the jar and refrigerate overnight or up to 12 hours. "Taste the next morning and if they are not sweet enough, add a little more sugar," says Dana. Serve immediately, while still cold.

Jestine's Kitchen

SALT

Bermuda

Fat Hen

3140 Maybank Highway, Johns Island
(843) 559-9090
thefathen.com
Executive Chef: Fred Neuville
Owners: Husband-and-wife team Fred and Joan Neuville

Follow your nose and the red chicken tracks on the front porch of this restaurant roost with Lowcountry/French Huguenot–inspired pluck. Fat Hen's "coop" has a convenient Johns Island address, situated virtually equidistant from downtown and the upscale resort barrier islands Kiawah and Seabrook. Congenial chef-owner Fred Neuville is a veteran chef and a graduate of the Culinary Institute of America. He draws heavily on French classical technique and the ingredients indigenous to the Lowcountry at Fat Hen—so named because Fred wanted something that evoked nurturing images and a French undertone. Plus, it's so much fun to say!

Fat Hen lays all kinds of golden dishes, and is a very popular spot for a particularly plucky Bloody Mary's with Sunday brunch. The sophisticated yet homey French country look and smashing food draw an eclectic, animated crowd. "Our price structure is such that we get the full gamut," says Fred. "People drink Bud Light and people drink Cristal Champagne."

His oyster recipe was something he created many years ago, as a young chef working at a French bistro in Richmond, Virginia. He resurrected it at Fat Hen because it was a natural fit with the restaurant's theme. "Oysters and country ham are very Lowcountry and the preparation ties in the French angle. The French have their hams, too," says Fred.

OYSTERS SAUTÉED WITH COUNTRY HAM AND WILD MUSHROOMS OVER GRILLED BREAD

(SERVES 4)

4 thick slices Tuscan or country-style bread
2 tablespoons olive oil
½ cup finely chopped shallots
½ cup dry white wine
3 egg yolks
¼ cup heavy cream
¾ cup sliced wild mushrooms (cremini, portobello, shiitake, or a combination)
¾ cup finely cubed aged and cured country ham
½ cup coarsely chopped fresh spinach
20 oysters, shucked
Salt and freshly ground black pepper to taste
Fresh parsley or thyme, chopped (optional)

Heat the oven broiler or grill. Brush both sides of the bread evenly with a thin coating of olive oil. Broil until lightly browned on both sides or grill until just charred. Set aside.

For the topping, heat a large sauté pan over high heat. Add the shallots and the wine and reduce by half. Meanwhile, in a small bowl, combine the egg yolks and heavy cream to create the "liaison." Reduce the heat to medium-low. Add the liaison, mushrooms, and country ham to the pan, and stir occasionally. Once the sauce has thickened and coats the back of a wooden spoon (about 4 minutes), add the spinach and the oysters to the pan. Sauté, stirring until the oysters just turn translucent and the spinach has wilted, about 3 minutes, depending on the size of the oysters. Season to taste with salt and pepper. Serve over the warm grilled bread, dividing the pan sauce evenly. If desired, garnish with parsley or thyme.

HUGUENOT HAVEN

During long stretches of the sixteenth and seventeenth centuries, Huguenots (French Protestants and members of the Reformed Church established in 1550 by John Calvin) were persecuted in their predominantly Catholic home country of France for following their beliefs. The tension and bloodshed reached an all-time high with Louis XIV's revocation of the Edict of Nantes (1685), which essentially called for the obliteration of the Huguenots. Those who could fled to safe havens, including the thousands who made it to the shores of America between 1618 and 1725. Charleston, unlike Quaker-rich Philadelphia and Puritan-rich Boston, was a religiously tolerant colony that welcomed virtually all religions and was a popular Huguenot immigration destination. The Huguenot legacy here is not a small one; it lives on in old Charleston family names, like Ravenel and Manigault, and in revered dishes, like Huguenot torte and pilau (Huguenot rice pilaf). Incidentally, the Charleston word for recipe ("receipt") is derived from the French equivalent recette.

Red Orchids China Bistro

1401 Sam Rittenberg Boulevard, West Ashley
(843) 573-8787
redorchids.com
Owners: Tony and Kelly Chu

Despite Red Orchid's humble exterior and non-glamorous suburban shopping mall setting, those who enter are treated to an emperor-worthy authentic Chinese dining experience in a decidedly no buffet zone. Husband-and-wife team Tony and Kelly Chu are both natives of China, and they succeed in making the customer number one and the food (with nods from Singapore, Hunan, Szechuan, Shanghai, and Guangzhou) beautifully plated and as good as it gets in these parts.

Tony rules the front of the house, happily sharing his friendly grace, expert knowledge, and collection of sake. Meanwhile, Kelly oversees the back of the house and is referred to as a "master saucer" because of her saucy sauce skills.

Known as *char siu bao* in Chinese, these divine bites of sweet and savory barbecued pork wrapped in a pillowy, dumpling-type dough can best be described as Chinese Sloppy Joes. "Barbecue is one of the many staples on hand at Chinese dim sum shops—which are something like coffee shops that serve tapas-like treats," says Tony. This delectable dish transports him to memories of his childhood, when he regularly supped on the buns with his family. In Tony's version, the dumplings are baked, but they can also be steamed.

Be patient with this recipe. It looks complicated and time-consuming, but if you break it down into three prep parts over the course of a day, it's not hard at all and well worth the effort.

Barbecue Pork Buns

(MAKES 16 BUNS)

For the barbecue pork:

2 pounds pork butt, cut into 1-inch cubes
1½ tablespoons each of dark soy sauce, light soy sauce, honey, and oyster sauce
2 tablespoons whiskey
3½ tablespoons hoisin sauce
½ teaspoon five-spice powder
¼ teaspoon salt
Pinch of freshly ground black pepper

For the barbecue sauce and filling:

1 tablespoon peanut or vegetable oil
⅔ cup chopped onion
1 cup of the roasted pork
2 teaspoons Chinese rice wine or sherry
4 teaspoons oyster sauce
1 teaspoon sesame oil
1½ teaspoons dark soy sauce
4 teaspoons ketchup
1 tablespoon granulated sugar
6 tablespoons chicken stock
Pinch of freshly ground black pepper

For the dough:

½ cup plus 2 tablespoons granulated sugar

⅔ cup warm water (around 75°F)

3 teaspoons dry active yeast

2⅔ cups high-gluten flour (look for flour labeled "best for bread machines")

½ cup (minus 2 tablespoons) peanut or vegetable oil

1 egg, beaten, for glazing

To prepare the barbecue pork, toss the pork with the remaining barbecue pork ingredients in a large bowl, working well with your hands to coat evenly. Marinate the pork, covered and refrigerated, for 4 hours or overnight. When ready to cook the pork, preheat the oven broiler and place the oven rack in the position second closest to the broiler. Remove the pork from the marinade (reserve the marinade for basting) and place it in a sturdy roasting pan. Broil for 8 minutes, baste with the marinade, and turn the meat. Repeat this for 20 or 30 minutes, basting and turning the meat every 8 minutes, or until the pork's interior is no longer pink and has reached an internal temperature of 170°F. Tony advises being extra careful not to let the sugar in the marinade char while broiling. Allow the pork to cool and refrigerate, covered, 4 hours or overnight. After the pork has rested, chop it coarsely to create small, Sloppy Joe–size pieces.

To make the sauce and the filling, reserve 1 cup of pork (keep the rest for a second batch or for another use). Heat the oil in a large sauté pan over medium heat. Add the onion and sauté, stirring, until golden brown, about 5 minutes. Add the reserved pork and the remaining sauce ingredients to the pan. Stir together and sauté for 5 minutes. Reduce the heat to low and simmer until the sauce has reduced to a thick and bubbly consistency. Cool and refrigerate 4 hours or overnight.

To prepare the dough, dissolve the sugar in the warm (not hot!) water in a large bowl. Add the yeast, stir gently, and set aside for 30 minutes to proof. When the mixture is foamy or light brown in color, it's ready. Add the flour and oil to the bowl. With

your hands, mix the ingredients together until cohesive. When the dough has formed a ball, remove it from the bowl and knead on a floured surface until smooth and elastic, about 5 minutes. Place the dough in a large, lightly oiled bowl and allow to rise for 4 hours covered loosely with a damp towel.

To make the bao balls, lightly flour a working surface and roll the dough out ¼ inch thick. With a 3-inch round cookie cutter, cut out 16 rounds of dough. To fill, scoop a tablespoon of the prepared filling into the center of each dough round. Pull two of the edges together toward the center to cover the filling, and pinch to seal. Turn the dough a quarter turn and pinch the other two edges together. Repeat twice, turning and pinching the edges, until the bun is sealed, twisting gently the fourth time to ensure that the bun is completely sealed. Repeat with the remaining dough rounds.

Arrange the buns 3 inches apart on a large baking sheet. Set aside to rest and rise until puffy, about 1 hour. Preheat the oven to 350°F. Brush the top of each bun with the beaten egg. Bake for 15–20 minutes or until golden brown. Serve immediately.

Monza

451 King Street, downtown
(843) 720-8787
monzapizza.com
Executive Chef: Brian Emery

The Ferrari of authentic Neapolitan-style pizza in greater Charleston, Monza reaches an edible finish line with Formula One fare and unparalleled pizza pizzazz. Named after a great Italian car racing track and decked with Italian trimmings, including vintage black-and-white photos of racing greats and a genuine Ferrari engine hoisted over a festive community table, Monza looks the sleek Speed Racer part. Tangerine-colored imported Italian tiles dress the walls, while shiny zebrawood tables swirl together like a giant bowl of ice cream, with warm chocolate and caramel wood tones.

Occupying the center of Monza's universe is a wood-burning oven that operates from 700°F up to 1,000°F and eternally emits fragrant white oak smoke. The aroma wafts temptingly down King Street, attracting loyal legions like bees to honey.

Executive chef Brian Emery worked five years of his young career at Monza before a recent promotion to head the kitchen. His dual chef mantra is consistency and simplicity and he is ever striving to "keep customers happy and making the good food we're known for."

The ultimate feel-good food, Monza's ricotta meatballs served in a fresh sauce laced with Italian sausage and red peppers is just the kind of food Monza's is known for and is a longtime menu staple. Don't forget fresh bread for dipping, and you've got a meal to remember all in one bowl.

ITALIAN SAUSAGE AND RICOTTA MEATBALLS WITH PEPPERS, ONIONS, AND TOMATO SAUCE

(SERVES 4–6)

For the sauce:

2 tablespoons extra-virgin olive oil
3 cups chopped onion
3 cups chopped red bell peppers
3 cloves garlic, minced
Salt and freshly ground black pepper to taste
1 cup red wine
2 cups pureed whole peeled canned tomatoes
4 cups hand-crushed whole peeled canned tomatoes

For the meatballs:

2 cups fresh bread crumbs (preferably from chewy, Tuscan-style bread)
½ cup ricotta cheese
½ cup whole milk
¼ cup chopped fresh flat-leaf parsley
1 large egg
¼ cup grated Parmesan cheese, plus more for garnish
1 pound Italian pork sausage, casings removed
Salt and freshly ground black pepper to taste
3 tablespoons finely chopped fresh parsley to garnish

To make the sauce, heat the olive oil in a large pot over medium heat. Add the onions and peppers and sauté, stirring, until softened, about 8 minutes. Add the garlic and continue to sauté until just softened, about 4 minutes. Season with salt and pepper. Increase heat to high and add the wine. Cook until reduced by about half and you can no longer smell the alcohol. Add the tomatoes and bring to a boil, then reduce to a simmer; continue simmering for another 10 minutes. Season to taste with salt and pepper.

Meanwhile, prepare the meatballs. Preheat the oven to 400°F. In a large bowl, combine the bread crumbs, ricotta, milk, parsley, egg, and Parmesan, mixing well to combine with a wooden spoon. Add the sausage and mix, using your hands, until combined. (Do not overwork the mixture once the sausage has been added, or the meatballs risk becoming tough.) Dampen your hands and begin forming golf ball–sized meatballs (approximately 2 ounces each; you should end up with about 16). The meatballs should be slightly sticky. If they are too dry, add a little more milk; if too wet, add a few more bread crumbs. Line a large baking sheet with parchment paper and evenly space the meatballs. Bake for 20 minutes or until they're golden brown and firm to the touch. Then add the meatballs to the sauce and simmer another 20 minutes.

Serve meatballs and sauce in shallow bowls and garnish with additional Parmesan cheese and a generous drizzle of chopped parsley. This is also delicious over your favorite cooked pasta.

Charleston Grill

224 King Street, downtown
(843) 577-4522
charlestongrill.com
Executive Chef: Michelle Weaver

After twelve years working alongside marquee chef Bob Waggoner, Michelle Weaver was given the chance in 2009 to step into the limelight as executive chef at Charleston Grill, where she's been working ever since.

Then, she was one of just a handful of female chefs leading the Charleston cooking show, and now there are several other prominent female chefs, as you'll see in the pages to follow. Weaver enthusiastically supports her female chef cohorts. "When I first took over the helm, I was the only chick in the boys' club. It's amazing to see all the women rocking so many kitchens now," she exclaims.

Weaver's four-tiered Pure, Lush, Cosmopolitan, and Southern menu was created to reflect the diversity at the Four Star AAA Diamond restaurant. "We needed Southern, simplistic food on the 'Southern' side, Bob's (referring to former executive chef Bob Waggoner) lush French flavors on the 'pure and lush' side, and something more forward-thinking with the 'cosmopolitan' side," says Michelle.

She credits her "amazing kitchen staff" and front of the house team, led by maestro general manager Mickey Bakst, for creating memorable experiences for guests, and of course, the guests who "keep coming back to let us be a part of their special night."

The relaxed elegance of the mahogany walls, cream-colored leather seating, and sashay of gossamer curtains in the dining room, the top-notch service, sexy, live jazz music, and an incredible wine list make Charleston Grill a premier destination for high-level dining or an easy night noshing at the sophisticated bar.

About her celebrated crab cakes, Weaver says they are all crab and no cake. "One bite is like tasting a mouthful of the Lowcountry."

CHARLESTON GRILL CRAB CAKE WITH CREEK SHRIMP AND LIME TOMATO VINAIGRETTE

(MAKES 4 (3-OZ.) FIRST COURSE CAKES OR 8–10 SMALLER, APPETIZER PORTIONS)

For the crab cakes:

½ cup mayonnaise

½ teaspoon kosher or sea salt

¼ teaspoon freshly ground white pepper

1 egg white

Zest from ½ lemon

Juice from ½ lemon

1 tablespoon finely chopped chives

1 tablespoon freshly chopped thyme leaves

1 pound lump blue crab meat, gently picked over to remove shells

2 tablespoons fresh bread crumbs made from crust-less white bread (about 2 slices) pulverized in a food processor fitted with a metal blade

1 tablespoon unsalted butter

2 tablespoons canola or vegetable oil

For the vinaigrette:

½ cup extra virgin olive oil

2 shallots, finely chopped

6 peeled, de-veined shrimp, cut into thin strips (julienne)

10 red (cherry, grape or pear) tomatoes

10 yellow (cherry, grape or pear) tomatoes

Juice of 2 limes

2 tablespoons finely chopped dill

Kosher or sea salt and freshly ground white pepper to taste

Whisk together the mayonnaise, salt, pepper, egg white, lemon zest, lemon juice, chives and thyme in a medium bowl. Gently, fold in the crab meat, being careful not to break up the flesh. Form into six evenly sized patties. Press all sides into the bread crumbs. (Note: The cakes can be formed, covered and refrigerated in a single layer over night or until ready to cook). To finish, heat the butter and oil together in a large skillet over medium high heat. Arrange the cakes in a single layer, evenly spaced. Cook until browned, about 3 minutes. Reduce heat to medium. Gently flip with a spatula and cook on the second side, about 2 minutes. Reserve warm.

To make the vinaigrette, place the oil in a medium skillet or sauce pan and heat over medium. Add the shallots and cook until softened, 2 minutes. Add the shrimp, stir, and cook until just opaque, 30 seconds. Add the remaining ingredients and cook another minute, or until just heated through. Taste and adjust seasoning as needed. Serve the warm sauce (about ¼ cup each cake) over the warm crab cakes. Serve immediately.

Peninsula Grill

112 North Market Street, downtown
(843) 723-0700
peninsulagrill.com
Executive Chef: Graham Dailey

Peninsula Grill feels a bit like a Southern gentlemen's club that wisely and graciously invites the ladies, on bent knee, to supper and later into the parlor (that is, bar) for a dandy of a mint julep and some romantic banter. Suave, swank, and debonair, Peninsula Grill is decorated with restrained Southern taste and hushed by soothing, slate-gray, velvet-lined walls and nineteenth-century portraits of celebrated Charlestonians. Intimate, with just one hundred seats in the dining area, Peninsula Grill (AAA Four Diamond) is one of Charleston's premier special occasion restaurants and one of her most revered. People come from near and far on birthdays, anniversaries, and other notable life occasions for elegant (but never prissy) new American cuisine with Southern influences.

Le Cordon Bleu (Paris) trained executive chef Graham Dailey has been with Peninsula Grill for many years in varying capacities, and has spent the last several as executive chef, honing the menu to match his increasing yen for simplicity honoring gorgeous products. "If you start with amazing (say, oysters) don't jumble it up. Keep things real," says Dailey.

Voila, his elegant (yet still very simple), oysters casino. They're a riff on a dish a former girlfriend's mother prepared for him a few years ago in Chatham, MA. "She just simplified everything and that was what made them so amazing."

A dedicated fisherman by day, he's a fan of Lady's Island deep cup oysters from the waters of the nearby ACE Basin. "The waters there are moving all the time and the oysters are consistently plum, juicy, briny, clean and salty. The absolute perfect oyster,'" he declares. If you can't find them, just get the freshest you can find where you are.

LADY'S ISLAND OYSTERS CASINO

(MAKES 3 DOZEN)

- ¾ cup diced cooked bacon
- 1 tablespoon unsalted butter
- ¾ cup minced green bell pepper
- ¾ cup minced red bell pepper
- ¾ cup minced shallot
- 3 tablespoons minced garlic
- 1½ cups thinly sliced green onion, white and green parts
- ¼ teaspoon kosher salt
- ¼ teaspoon white pepper
- 1½ cups panko-style breadcrumbs
- 3 tablespoons minced chives
- ¼ teaspoon hot sauce
- 36 oysters (Lady's Island Oysters Preferred)
- Rock salt
- Lemon wedges for garnish

In a large skillet, combine the bacon and butter over medium heat, and cook until butter is melted. Add the green bell pepper, red bell pepper, shallot and garlic. Cook, stirring occasionally, until the vegetables are soft, 6–8 minutes. Stir in the green onion, salt, pepper and breadcrumb, and set aside to cool for 20 minutes. Stir in the chives and hot sauce.

Preheat the oven to 400°F.

Pour enough rock salt onto a large sheet pan to evenly cover the bottom. Shuck the oysters, detaching them from the shell but leaving them on the half shell. Arrange the oysters on the rock salt. Place a heaping spoonful of the cooled breadcrumb and bell pepper mixture onto each oyster. Bake until golden brown, 8–10 minutes. Remove from the oven.

To serve, place fresh rock salt on a serving platter. Arrange the warm oysters on salt, and garnish with lemon wedges.

THE ACE BASIN

The basin is located along the southern half of South Carolina's Atlantic coastline, stretching the 70 mile span between Charleston and Beaufort. It is named after the three major rivers that drain into the area: the Ashepoo, the Combahee, and the Edisto Rivers. These rivers drain primarily into the St. Helena Sound, which drains into the Atlantic Ocean. The 350,000 acre basin hosts a pristine preserve of wetlands, marshes, hardwood forests, fauna and riverine systems. The waters constantly flush and move, which helps to create the pure, "perfect" oyster which Peninsula Grill's Executive Chef Graham Dailey and many Charleston area chefs so passionately utilize in their kitchens.

The Boathouse Restaurant

The Boathouse at Breach Inlet
101 Palm Boulevard, Isle of Palms
(843) 886-8000
boathouserestaurants.com
Executive Chef: Mike Eckert

After years of cultivating relationships with local fishermen, the kitchen staff at The Boathouse at Breach Inlet has amassed an armada of trawling-free, sustainable local fisherman contacts, ensuring only the freshest local finds show up at the kitchen door every morning. Twenty-something, enthusiastic and talented executive chef Mike Eckert picked up the importance of freshness from mentor and former Boathous executive chef, Charles Arena.

Eckert continues to source from local, sustainable fishermen (especially celebrated Abundant Seafood), and operates with the perspective that "simplicity is bliss." He likes to let the food speak for itself and approaches his cooking with precision and simplicity.

The views from The Boathouse are stunning. Breach Inlet cuts into the Atlantic, creating a dramatic and frothy maritime vista, made even more beautiful by the spectacular Lowcountry sunsets. As much a family restaurant as a spot-on destination for romantic dining, it's a strong dining magnet for tourists and locals alike.

The following recipe is a long-standing best-seller at The Boathouse. Eckert has left it virtually unchanged since its early days on the restaurant's menu. Once you try it, you'll understand why. The extra good news is that the fritters are surprisingly easy to make.

CRAB FRITTERS WITH MILD GREEN TABASCO CREAM SAUCE

(MAKES ABOUT 24 FRITTERS OR 6 SERVINGS)

For the fritters:

1 cup Duke's Mayonnaise
1 teaspoon Old Bay Seasoning
Juice of ½ lemon
1 tablespoon dried parsley
1 egg
Salt and freshly ground black pepper to taste
¼ pound lump crabmeat
¼ pound jumbo lump crabmeat
¼ pound crab claw meat
1 cup panko bread crumbs plus ½ cup for coating
4 tablespoons canola or vegetable oil

For the cream sauce:

Juice of 1 lemon
2 cups white wine
3 tablespoons rice wine vinegar
1 shallot, minced
1 5-ounce bottle Tabasco Green Pepper Sauce
1 quart (4 cups) heavy cream
3 tablespoons cornstarch
Salt and freshly ground black pepper to taste

For garnish:

¼ cup finely chopped fresh parsley

Begin by prepping the fritters. In a large bowl, combine the mayonnaise, Old Bay Seasoning, lemon juice, dried parsley, egg, salt, and pepper, whisking until smooth. Thoroughly pick over the crabmeat and remove any shells or hard shards. Add all crabmeat to the mayonnaise mixture and fold in with a wooden spoon, stirring to combine. Stir in 1 cup of the panko bread crumbs until evenly combined. Refrigerate for 30 minutes to set the fritter mixture.

Meanwhile, prepare the cream sauce. Combine the lemon juice, white wine, rice wine vinegar, and shallot in a medium saucepan. Bring to a boil over high heat. Reduce by half, or until about 1 cup of liquid remains. Add the Tabasco and cream, bring to a boil, and reduce to a simmer. In a small bowl, combine the cornstarch with enough cool water (roughly 3–4 tablespoons) to liquefy it, forming a slurry. Stir until a smooth, loose paste forms. Add the paste to the sauce, whisking to combine. Simmer the sauce gently until it is thick enough to coat the back of a spoon, about 10 minutes. Season to taste with salt and pepper.

Next, shape and cook the fritters. Using your hands or a small scoop, shape the cooled fritter mixture into 1-ounce balls. You should be able to make about 24. Place the reserved ½ cup panko bread crumbs in a small bowl. Roll each of the fritters gently in the crumbs to coat evenly. Heat the oil in a cast-iron pan or heavy-bottomed frying pan over medium heat. When sizzling, arrange the fritters in a single layer in the pan and fry until golden brown, about 3 minutes. You may need to work in batches. Turn each fritter and fry on the other side. Remove fritters from the pan with a slotted spoon and drain on paper towels. Season lightly with salt and pepper.

To serve, spoon about ¼ cup of the sauce on each of six plates, spreading to form a pool. Top with 4 fritters and garnish each with a drizzle of chopped fresh parsley. Serve immediately.

PUT UP YOUR DUKE'S!

No self-respecting Southern chef, home cook or otherwise, would settle for anything less than Duke's Mayonnaise in his or her condiment pantry. When I first moved to South Carolina, a Charleston-raised pal shrieked upon seeing Hellmann's in my refrigerator. Duke's roots go back to Greenville, South Carolina (about a four-hour drive northwest of Charleston), where it was created by Eugenia Duke in 1917. Duke's was raised in the South and its ingredient list does not contain sugar, giving it a flavor tang unlike that of many other commercial brands. Duke's, it could (and will) be heatedly argued, can only be bested by homemade mayonnaise.

Langdon's Restaurant & Wine Bar

778 South Shellmore Boulevard, Mount Pleasant
(843) 388-9200
langdonsrestaurant.com
Chef/Owner: Patrick Owens

Patrick Owens's path to restaurant success was less than conventional. It included high school football, multiple road trips playing guitar with a band called No Wake, and a degree in marketing from Clemson University. What it did not include was formal culinary training. That proved to be no matter for the restaurant maverick and Mount Pleasant native, who cut his cooking baby teeth at numerous restaurants before opening Langdon's in 2003. A smashing success since day one, Langdon's is a surprise treat tucked into a strip mall and has garnered multiple AAA Four Diamond ratings and the adoration of foodies. A bona fide white linen restaurant with a neat black and white color scheme, Langdon's is a cosmopolitan culinary enclave of Patrick's own talented making. "I like to find what looks really good and try to put it together without it being too far out there," he says.

The spring rolls recipe to follow (no longer a regular on the menu), was a number-one seller over the years. It is so delicious and beautiful that I decided to keep the recipe in this revised cookbook.

The rolls can be prepared ahead and frozen for a month or two before frying and serving. The avocado cream, however, is highly perishable and needs to be prepared within an hour or two of serving.

LOBSTER AND AVOCADO SPRING ROLLS WITH ASIAN VEGETABLES, SPICY CHILI SAUCE, AND AVOCADO CREAM

(MAKES 30 SPRING ROLLS OR 6 APPETIZER PORTIONS)

For the spring rolls:

6 tablespoons olive oil
2 red peppers, seeded and finely sliced
2 yellow peppers, seeded and finely sliced
1 large red onion, finely sliced
4 tablespoons finely minced garlic
4 tablespoons sesame oil
4 tablespoons finely chopped minced ginger
3 cups finely sliced napa cabbage
2 carrots, peeled and finely shredded
Generous dash each of soy sauce, rice wine vinegar, honey, and Sriracha (a spicy Thai condiment available in most grocery stores)
Salt and freshly ground black pepper to taste
½ cup finely chopped fresh cilantro, plus more for serving
2 tablespoons toasted sesame seeds
3 1-pound Maine lobsters
4 avocados, sliced ¼ inch thick
30 spring roll wrappers
1 egg
2 cups peanut oil for frying

For the avocado cream:

1 avocado

Juice of 1 lime

½ cup half-and-half

3 tablespoons heavy cream

Salt and freshly ground white pepper to taste

To prepare the spring rolls, begin by heating 3 tablespoons of olive oil in a large sauté pan over medium-high heat. Add the sliced red and yellow peppers and red onion to the pan, stir, and sauté until just softened, about 5 minutes. Just as the peppers are nearing completion, add 2 tablespoons each of garlic, sesame oil, and fresh ginger. Set aside the pepper mixture. Meanwhile, heat another 3 tablespoons of olive oil over medium-high heat in a large sauté pan. Sauté the cabbage until softened, 7–8 minutes. Drain off any excess liquid and set aside. In a large bowl, combine the pepper and onion mixture, the cabbage, and the raw carrots, soy sauce, rice wine vinegar, honey, and Sriracha. Season to taste with salt and pepper, mix thoroughly, cover, and refrigerate overnight. The following day, put the mixture in a large kitchen towel or cheesecloth and twist, over a sink, to squeeze out all excess liquid. Add the fresh cilantro and toasted sesame seeds to the mixture. Set aside.

Fill a large pot or a stockpot three-quarters full, salt generously, and bring up to a rolling boil over high heat. Add the live lobsters, cover, and cook for 2 minutes. Then shock the lobsters by placing them in a deep ice water bath until they are cold. Crack the lobster claws and tails, remove the meat, and coarsely chop. (The flesh will be "quite rare," according to Patrick.) Combine the lobster in a medium bowl with the remaining 2 tablespoons each of garlic, sesame oil, and fresh ginger.

To begin "spring roll perfection" (as Patrick describes these little gems), place 1 tablespoon of the vegetable mixture in the center of each spring roll wrapper. Top each with a couple chunks of lobster and a slice of avocado. (You'll want to slice the avocados just before assembling the rolls, or they will discolor.) Roll the wrappers into tight, cigarlike packages, tucking the ends into the roll to seal. Beat the egg in a small bowl and brush the top of each roll with a thin layer of egg wash. Line the rolls up in a single layer on a cookie sheet and refrigerate until ready to fry.

To prepare the avocado cream, puree the avocado, lime juice, and half-and-half in the bowl of a food processor until smooth. Slowly stream in the heavy cream through the mouth of the processor bowl while the motor is running. Season with salt and white pepper to taste and strain by pressing the mixture through a fine-mesh strainer. Set aside.

To fry the spring rolls, heat the peanut oil in a deep skillet over medium-high heat. When it has reached 350°F, add the spring rolls in batches (do not crowd!) and fry until they are golden brown and floating to the top of the skillet. Serve 5 rolls per plate, topping with a generous dollop of the avocado cream, a drizzle of sriracha, and some sprigs of fresh cilantro.

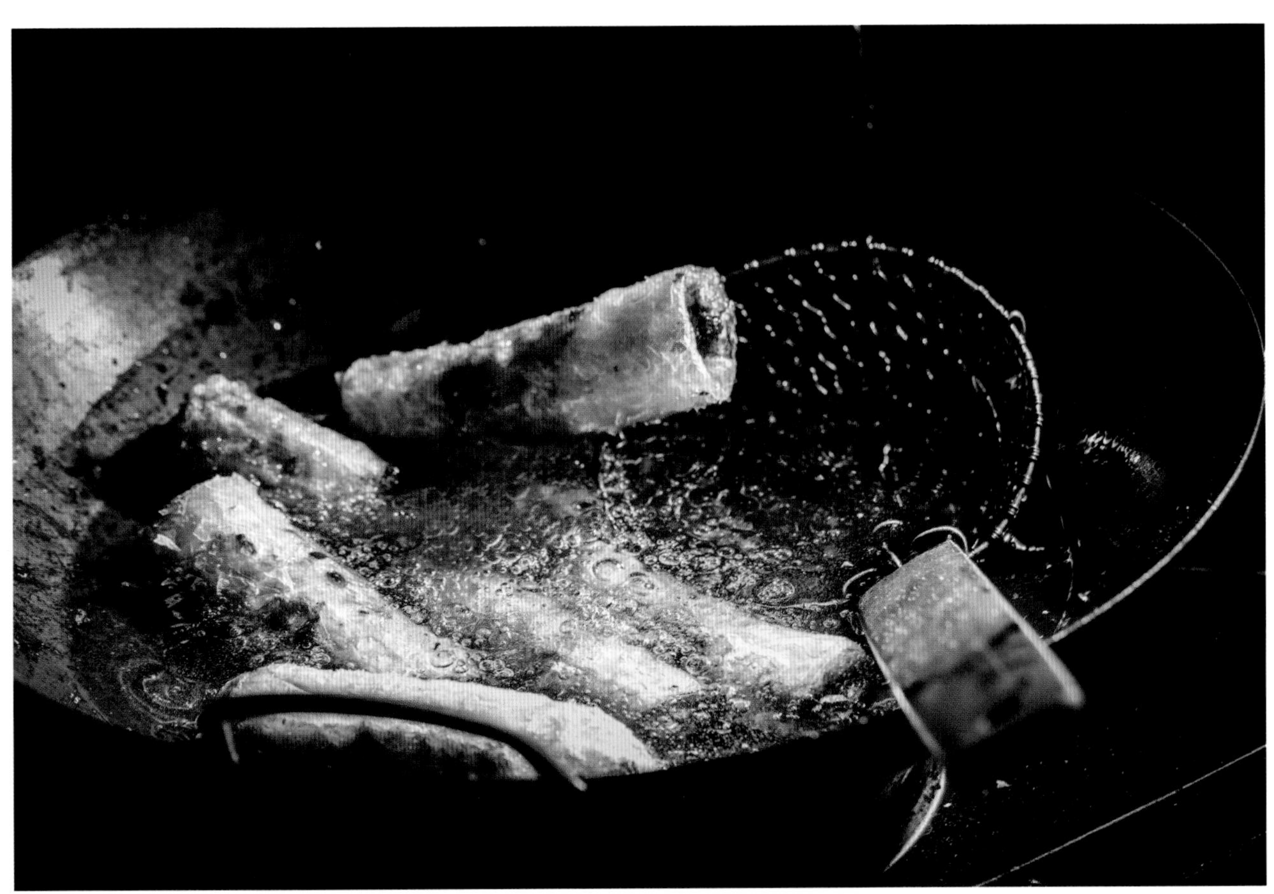

Pavilion Bar

225 East Bay Street (at the Market Pavilion Hotel), downtown
(843) 266-4222
marketpavilion.com
Executive Chef: Demetre Castanas

The Pavilion Bar is a luxe rooftop hot spot with open views of the Cooper River and Charleston Harbor. The restaurant boasts sexy, sophisticated eats from a staggering Tuna Tower and Spicy Tandoori Chicken Salad to the decadent Duck Confit Nachos featured here.

The upscale hotel is a popular wedding reception destination. And it's likely that more than one of those weddings was conceived with a proposal at this ultraromantic, cosmopolitan spot, with sweeping waterfront vistas and an azure blue swimming pool with a gurgling waterfall.

An enforced dress code and the cosmopolitan menu ensure a steady stream of interesting people views, too. Enjoying fun, light fare while sipping one of the restaurant's specialty drinks (Paviliontini, anyone?) on a warm, breezy Charleston evening is tough to beat—especially if you manage to avoid falling in the swimming pool from the sheer giddiness of it all.

This recipe has it all—ooey gooey cheese, the round, earthy flavors of duck confit, the kick of peppery heat, and sweet fruit.

DUCK CONFIT NACHOS WITH RED ONIONS, TOMATOES, PINEAPPLE SALSA, AND BLUE CORN TORTILLA CHIPS

(SERVES 4)

For the duck confit:

4 duck breasts, skin-on
¼ cup coarse salt (preferably sea salt or kosher salt)
1 bay leaf
3 cloves garlic
3 sprigs fresh thyme
4 cups duck fat (available online or at specialty stores), cold or at room temperature

For the salsa:

1 cup diced fresh pineapple
½ cup diced red onion
½ cup seeded and diced red bell pepper
½ cup finely chopped fresh cilantro
Salt and freshly ground black pepper to taste

For the queso sauce:

1 stick (¼ pound) butter
¼ cup diced shallot
¼ cup seeded and diced jalapeños
¼ cup all-purpose flour
1 pint heavy cream
2 cups shredded Monterey Jack cheese
Salt and freshly ground black pepper to taste

For serving:

About 4 cups best-quality blue corn tortilla chips

Prepare the confit several weeks in advance (it will store well, refrigerated) or at least 12 hours before assembling the entire dish. Preheat the oven to 250°F. Toss all of the confit ingredients together in a sturdy medium roasting pan, coating the duck

breasts evenly. Arrange the duck breasts in a single layer in the pan, cover the pan tightly with aluminum foil, and cook for 12–14 hours. Remove from the oven and allow to cool. Pull the duck breasts apart into chunky strips with your fingers, covering the duck with rendered fat, and return to the pan, cover the pan, and refrigerate to store. (You will need 1 cup of the confit for this recipe. Save the rest for another use.)

To prepare the salsa, combine all the salsa ingredients in a medium bowl, tossing to mix. Taste and adjust salt and pepper as needed. Cover and let salsa stand at room temperature for 1 hour to develop the flavors or refrigerate overnight. Bring the salsa to room temperature before serving to maximize the flavor and to keep the nachos good and hot. (This makes more salsa than you will need. The remainder is great as a dip for leftover chips—if there are any.)

To prepare the queso sauce, melt the butter over medium heat and add the shallot and jalapeños. Sauté until softened, about 3 minutes. Reduce the heat to low. Add the flour and whisk vigorously for about 8 minutes, or until the roux has thickened and has no visible lumps. Increase the heat to medium-high, add the cream, and bring to a low simmer, whisking constantly. Once the sauce is thickened and gently bubbling, add the cheese and stir to melt. Add salt and pepper as needed.

The dish can be served on individual plates or on a platter. Just before serving, reheat 1 cup of confit in a pan over low heat. Toss the duck (discard any excess fat) with the chips in a large bowl. Arrange in a mound and drizzle generously with the queso sauce. Top with a few dollops of the salsa.

Fleet Landing

186 Concord Street, downtown
(843) 722-8100
fleetlanding.net
Owners: Tradd and Weesie Newton
Executive Chef: Drew Hedlund

Housed in a former World War II U.S. Navy debarkation station, Fleet Landing maintains the unique distinction on this water-wrapped peninsula of being the only restaurant of note that actually sits on the water's edge. Unobstructed views of Charleston's picturesque harbor combined with the restaurant's casual, maritime mood and eclectic menu of Southern staples and seafood make Fleet a go-to place, especially on gorgeous sunny days or warm, breezy nights, when the restaurant's food suits the mood.

Owners Tradd and Weesie Newton had the insight and guts to transform this long-deserted building into their dream, draping it with nautical nuances from life jackets to rope, while maintaining its original austere lines. The effect is winning and pairs well with executive chef Drew Hedlund's uncomplicated and well-balanced menu.

A fisherman himself, Drew draws on the inspiration of local waters and local produce to create a weekly "locavore" meal, but he doesn't shy away from beefy burgers or a rib-eye topped with house-made pimiento cheese. The golf ball–sized hush puppies, stuffed with a seafood and vegetable velouté, are a house favorite. Stuffing them halfway through the cooking process can be a bit of a challenge, but it's worth the effort. The filling is a big tasty surprise in the center of these fluffy fried delights. High-quality prepared lobster and crab stocks, as well as hush puppy mix, save time and can be purchased at most grocery stores. Don't scrimp on the seafood, however—remember to buy local and fresh whenever possible!

FLEET LANDING STUFFED HUSH PUPPIES

(MAKES 12 LARGE PUPPIES OR 6 APPETIZER PORTIONS)

For the sauce:

3 cups heavy cream

2½ cups water

2 cups lobster stock

1 cup crab stock

Salt and freshly ground black pepper to taste

4 sticks (1 pound) plus 2 tablespoons unsalted butter

3 ears fresh corn, shucked and kernels cut from the cobs

3 leeks (white parts only), well washed and finely julienned

3½ cups all-purpose flour

1½ teaspoons Old Bay Seasoning

Pinch of cayenne pepper

Pinch of freshly ground white pepper

¼ teaspoon ground cumin

1 one-pound box best-quality hush puppy mix (you will probably need eggs and milk, depending on the brand selected)

4 cups peanut oil

12 large (26–30 count) shrimp, peeled and deveined

2 cups fresh lobster meat

½ cup white wine

Fresh parsley, chopped (optional)

Begin by preparing the velouté sauce. In a large pot, bring the cream, water, lobster and crab stock, and salt and pepper to a low boil over high heat. In the meantime, melt 1 pound of butter in a large soup pot or stockpot over medium-high heat. Add the corn kernels and leeks to the melted butter pot, stirring, and cook over medium heat until both vegetables are just softened, about 5 minutes. Add the flour all at once, stirring to coat the vegetables evenly. Cook for about 3 minutes, and then gradually incorporate the simmering cream and stock mixture, stirring well to avoid lumps. Add the Old Bay Seasoning, cayenne pepper, white pepper, and cumin. Stir to incorporate, then reduce the heat to low and simmer the velouté until it is thick enough to coat the back of a spoon, about 12 minutes.

Meanwhile, prepare the hush puppy batter according to the manufacturer's directions. Heat the peanut oil to 350°F in a fryer or a deep skillet. Once the oil is hot, scoop the batter, using a large ice-cream scoop, into the oil. Fry until the hush puppies are about one quarter of the way done, about 2 minutes. Remove from the fryer and drain on paper towels. When they are cool enough to handle, cut a small piece off the bottom of each puppy with a serrated knife. This will create a steady base for the puppy to sit on. Next, cut a ¼-inch-thick slice off the top of each, and with a small fork, gently remove the raw batter in the center, leaving a sturdy ¼-inch-thick wall. Set the puppies and their tops aside.

Melt the remaining 2 tablespoons of butter over medium heat in a large pot. Add the shrimp and lobster. Sauté, tossing, until the seafood is almost translucent, about 4 minutes. Deglaze the pot with the white wine and reduce until the wine forms a glaze, about 1 minute. Add the simmering vegetable velouté sauce and stir. Taste and adjust salt and pepper as needed.

Return the cored hush puppies (but not the tops) to the hot (350°F) oil and fry until completely cooked and golden, another 5 or 6 minutes. Remove with a slotted spoon and briefly drain on paper towels. Using a small soup spoon, fill each puppy with velouté and replace the reserved tops. Serve immediately, placing 2 hush puppies on each shallow plate. Garnish, if desired, with a sprinkle of fresh chopped parsley.

Rita's Seaside Grille

2 Center Street, Folly Beach (on James Island)
(843) 588-2525
ritasseasidegrille.com
Executive Chef: Billy Spencer

Situated literally on the edge of what is alternatively deemed "The Edge of America" (or simply Folly Beach), Rita's is just a stone's throw from the frothy, popular surfing waters of the Atlantic. Its breezy, beachy locale lends itself both to the mood and look of the place, as well as the hefty, gutsy menu options, which include breakfast, lunch, and dinner every day of the week, and a very popular brunch on Saturday and Sunday.

Though casual, Rita's also retains a kind of muted elegance that comes through its captain chairs, high, glossy wood bars and tables. Beyond beach chic, it's a great stop before or after the beach, or anytime your belly is aching and in search of a good time. And, your canine pal(s) are welcome on the covered outdoor patio, which also houses some great live bands every night of the week.

Executive chef Billy Spencer has been at the helm here since Hall Management Group (of Slightly North of Broad, High Cotton, Halls Chophouse, and Old Village Post House Inn fame), bought it a few years ago. The Johnson & Wales grad describes Rita's crab dip, which was originally inspired by a restaurant where he worked in Florida, as "creamy, but not too heavy." It's rife with crab meat that he sources from a fisherman in North Carolina and as he points out, each portion if roughly 50 percent chock-full of crab. It's lovely that it can be made ahead and re-heated just before serving. Perfect game day fare!

Rita's Warm Blue Crab Dip

(MAKES 4–6 APPETIZER PORTIONS)

For the dip:

1½ cups cream cheese

½ cup heavy cream

2 tablespoons fresh Italian parsley, finely chopped

2 tablespoons fresh basil, cut into strips or a chiffonade

2 cups claw crabmeat

1½ teaspoons Worcestershire

½ teaspoon Tabasco

½ cup shredded cheddar cheese

¼ cup roasted, drained and finely diced red peppers

1½ tablespoons finely chopped fresh garlic

¼ cup fresh lemon juice

Kosher salt and freshly ground black pepper to taste

¼ cup grated cheddar cheese for garnish

Serve with tortilla chips, as shown here, or these dipping chips:

Two 6-inch pitas, each cut into eight wedges

1 tablespoon olive oil

Generous sprinkling kosher or sea salt and freshly ground black pepper

Melt the cream cheese and heavy cream together in a medium saucepan over medium heat, stirring until smooth. Pour into a medium bowl and set aside to cool. Fold the remaining ingredients into the cream mixture, stirring gently to combine. Taste and adjust seasoning as needed. Portion out into six microwave-proof ramekins or small bowls. (Note: The dip can be prepared ahead, covered and refrigerated up to a day in advance).

Meanwhile, prepare the chips. Preheat oven to 400° F. Toss together the pita wedges with the olive oil, salt and pepper. Arrange in a single layer, and toast until golden brown (tossing once or twice) about 12–15 minutes. Reserve warm.

To warm the dip "cups," microwave, uncovered, on high for one minute. Sprinkle each bowl with the cheddar cheese garnish and broil under a hot broiler until melted, just before serving. Serve warm with freshly prepared, warm chips.

Magnolias

185 East Bay Street, downtown
(843) 577-7771
magnolias-blossom-cypress.com
Founding Executive Chef: Donald Barickman
Culinary Operations: Don Drake
Executive Chef: Kelly Franz

Donald Barickman is widely recognized as one of the leaders of Charleston's first restaurant culinary renaissance, which most agree began with the opening of Magnolias shortly after the calamity that was Hurricane Hugo in 1989. Ironically, the storm put Charleston on the national awareness map. Donald, a young chef and recent Culinary Institute of America grad at the time, turned heads and dropped jaws with his groundbreaking notion of serving grits—widely considered breakfast fare—all day long in a white linen restaurant. And he had the audacity to cook them with stock, cream, and butter.

Creative work with Southern staples like rice, grits, corn, and beans, remains at the heart of the restaurant. These days the kitchen is run by a talented executive chef, Kelly Franz. Starting at Magnolias in 2003, she believes that consistency is the key to the restaurant's success. Franz stays true to the menu staples (like the fried green tomatoes) that many come to Magnolias to enjoy, while continuing to expand the menu with seasonally driven trends. "Magnolias has been home to me for over 13 years. I began working (here) in my second year of culinary school and have grown up in [this] kitchen with many of my coworkers alongside me. I am blessed to have found a restaurant that believes in creativity and tradition," says Franz.

Loyal patrons populate the pretty, spacious restaurant decorated with swaths of the forged iron magnolias for which it's named.

Culinary Operations Chef, Don Drake, also with the restaurant since its beginning, said the following Magnolias favorite came about from an overabundance of green tomatoes. "We tried out fried green tomatoes as a special. The recipe evolved from the tomatoes first being served with a rémoulade to the dish it is today. We thought the creaminess of the grits would be a nice contrast to the crunch of a fried green tomato, the country ham added some saltiness and the tomato chutney a touch of sweetness," says Drake.

Make the tomato chutney a day or several ahead. Prepare the grits and finish the fried tomatoes, ham, and tomato butter while the grits are cooking.

FRIED GREEN TOMATOES WITH CARAMELIZED ONION AND WHITE CHEDDAR GRITS, COUNTRY HAM AND TOMATO CHUTNEY

(MAKES 6 SERVINGS)

3 cups seasoned all-purpose flour (salt and pepper added to taste)

3 cups buttermilk

3 eggs

2 cups panko bread crumbs

¾ cup yellow cornmeal

⅓ cup julienned basil

18 slices green tomatoes, ¼ inch thick, about 5 whole tomatoes

4 cups canola oil

Tomato Chutney (recipe follows)

Caramelized Onion & White Cheddar Grits (recipe follows)

Tomato Butter (recipe follows)

6 (1½ ounce) slices of country ham, halved

This is a standard breading procedure that can be used for frying many kinds of vegetables. You'll need three separate containers or use three large freezer bags to save time on the cleanup. Place the seasoned flour in the first container or bag. In the second, mix the buttermilk and eggs together. In the third, mix the panko, cornmeal and basil. Evenly coat all tomatoes in the seasoned flour, shaking off the excess. Place in the buttermilk mixture, remove the tomatoes and shake off any excess. Place them in the final container of panko-cornmeal mixture, making sure to coat them well. (As you work to coat the tomatoes, try to keep one hand dry and use your other hand for the wet steps.)

In a large skillet or deep fryer, heat the canola oil to 325°F and fry the tomatoes in small batches until golden brown, about 3–4 minutes. Place on a paper towel to drain and keep warm.

For the tomato chutney:

2 cups granulated sugar

1 cup apple cider vinegar

3 cups julienned tomatoes, drained

1 cup julienned yellow onions

1 tablespoon minced jalapeno

1 teaspoons red pepper flakes

Place sugar and vinegar in heavy-bottomed sauce-pot over medium-high heat and bring to a boil. Reduce the heat to a simmer and reduce the volume by half. Add remaining ingredients and cook an hour or so until it becomes syrup-like. Remember that it will thicken as it cools. After it cooks down, remove from heat and cool. (Note: This will make more chutney than you need for this recipe. Store in the refrigerator up to several weeks in sealed container).

For the grits:

3 cups water

1 cup stone ground grits

½ cup heavy cream

1 small onion, julienned and caramelized in a small skillet with 1 teaspoon butter (Cook over medium high heat until golden brown).

1 cup grated white cheddar cheese

Kosher or coarse sea salt and pepper to taste

In a heavy-bottomed pot, bring the water to boil. Slowly stir in the grits and stir continuously for the first 5 minutes to prevent lumps. Turn the heat down to low and simmer for 30 minutes. Add the heavy cream and cook for 15 minutes more. The grits should be thick and plump, add more water or heavy cream if needed. Add the caramelized onion and white cheddar cheese. Cook 5 minutes more. Season to taste with coarse sea salt and pepper. Keep warm until ready to serve.

For the tomato butter:

1 tablespoon olive oil

3 shallots

1 cup tomato juice

¼ cup whipping cream

3 sticks unsalted butter, cut into small pieces

¼ teaspoon salt

Pinch ground white pepper

Warm the olive oil in a heavy-bottomed saucepot over medium-high heat. Sauté the shallots until translucent. Add the tomato juice and reduce until it becomes bubbly and thick. Add the cream and reduce until thickened, stirring often. Turn the heat down and, stirring constantly, add the butter a little bit at a time until all is incorporated. Remove from heat and hold in a warm area until ready to serve.

Putting it together:

Choose any good country ham and allow 1½ ounces or pieces of thinly sliced ham per person. Sear the ham in a sauté pan. Place 6 appetizer size plates on the counter and in the center of each plate place a 3-ounce scoop of caramelized onion and white cheddar grits. Starting with a single slice of fried green tomato, top the grits with alternate slices of tomato and ham. Finish the stack with a slice of tomato. Crown the stack with a spoonful of tomato chutney. Finish the dish using a 2-ounce ladle to drizzle tomato butter around the outside of the plate.

LITTLE JACK'S TAVERN

710 King Street, upper peninsula
(843) 531-6868
littlejackstavern.com
Neighbourhood, LLC Culinary Director: John Amato

The latest cousin to this restaurant group (which also owns Monza, page 9, and Leon's, page 46), that has just the right knack for getting its restaurants' concept, décor, menu and deliciousness fully aligned, Little Jack's Tavern may be the best of the bunch. That is saying a lot, trust me.

Named after a fictional boxer "Jack" who moved to Charleston in the 1940's when his prized boxing career ended, it embodies the mood and spirit of the American dream with a Big Apple spin. Soft and cozy, the banquettes are comfortably padded with horse-motif fabric cushions. At the center of it all is a bold, red bar with cubbies for housing all kinds of magnificent-looking Rat Pack-era cocktails served in sexy glasses by even sexier bartenders.

On the menu, largely created by super-talent John Amata (a Johnson & Wales grad with previous stints at FIG (page 38), running a food truck/catering company, Park Cafe, and with Neighbourhood, LLC), expect a slew of nostalgic goodies including big, juicy steaks; the diminutive, flavor-packed, and dangerously addictive Tavern burger; a tender shrimp burger; and Amato's excellent riff on steak tartare.

"The tarter is simple, tasty food and consistent. It's a great dish for sharing. It's not a classic with Dijon, olive oil, and the raw egg. It's more of a steakhouse style, classic French with caper vinaigrette, herbs, fish sauce, and red wine vinegar. The end result is a creamy type texture that we top with fried potato strings that we buy in bulk at the grocery store," says Amato. Simply delicious, just like everything at Little Jack's Tavern.

LITTLE JACK'S STEAK TARTARE

(SERVES 4)

For the dressing:

2 egg yolks

¼ cup red wine vinegar

2 tablespoons Lingham's Hot Sauce (substitute another brand if need be)

2 tablespoons freshly squeezed lemon juice

Pinch red pepper flakes

½ cup extra virgin olive oil

¼ cup fish sauce

For the tartare:

1 tablespoon finely chopped fresh parsley

1 tablespoon coarsely chopped fresh tarragon

1 tablespoon finely minced shallot or onion

1 6-ounce beef tenderloin

½ teaspoon kosher salt

½ teaspoon freshly ground black pepper

2 heaping tablespoons of prepared tartare dressing

1 teaspoon capers

For the garnish:

Drizzle grated Pecorino Romano

Drizzle extra virgin olive oil

Handful Pik Nik Brand Potato Sticks (available on the chip aisle in most grocery stores)

Wrap the tenderloin fot the tartare (recipe) in plastic wrap, and put in the freezer for at least 30 minutes to an hour to make extremely cold, but not frozen completely.

Prepare the dressing. Put all ingredients except the olive oil and fish sauce into a blender. Blend on low speed, while very slowly drizzling in about half of the olive oil. Turn the blender up to a medium speed and continue to add the olive oil until the emulsion gets thick and creamy. Once all of the oil is added, then add the fish sauce in two stages and blend to combine. Dressing is finished. Place in fridge until chilled, about an hour. (Note: The dressing can be prepared several hours in advance of combining with the beef).

For the tartare, cut the fresh onions and herbs and set aside. Remove the beef from the freezer and, using a very sharp knife, dice into ¼-inch cubes or smaller. Place the diced meat into a bowl. Add the salt, pepper, and dressing, and mix gently to combine. Add the capers, reserved chopped onion/shallot and herbs, and mix well to fully distribute all of the ingredients. Do not over work the meat.

Serve immediately. Arrange the tartare on a serving dish and drizzle lightly with the olive oil and grated cheese. Finish with a handful of potato sticks. Serve with a spoon for sharing.

Salads

Between the growing season that hardly ever sleeps and the thriving South Carolina agricultural industry, fruits, vegetables, and the stuff of salads have been principal players in Charleston kitchens since colonial times. A frugal, seasonally attuned lot, Charlestonians and Charleston chefs increasingly turn to the area's many local farmers and the verdant bins of local farmers' markets for inspiration. The first blush of spring ushers in young baby lettuces, spinach, and sweet onions, followed by the plump blueberries, raspberries, and peaches of summer. With the chill of autumn apples arrive from North Carolina and the South's siren call of greens—including mustard, collard, turnip, and kale.

FIG's executive chef Jason Stanhope's utterly simple arugula salad tossed with slivers of nutty, aged pecorino canestrato cheese and the lightest kiss of fresh lemon juice and fruity olive oil showcases his James Beard-winning balance of restraint and artistry using the freshest produce of the season. Two distinctly different, but equally delicious, versions of another beloved Charleston mainstay—chicken salad—make a splashy showing at Cru Cafe and The Glass Onion. And, we take a petite trip to France at Cafe Framboise with a sample of their memorable salad Niçoise.

FIG

232 Meeting Street, downtown
(843) 805-5900
eatatfig.com
Chef and Partner: Mike Lata
Manager and Partner: Adam Nemirow
Executive Chef: Jason Stanhope

FIG's chef/partner Mike Lata's regular rotations of FIG's menu to match the changes in the Lowcountry's produce and fishing seasons, combined with impeccable classic technique, yielding unfettered, unforgettable fare earned him national acclaim. He grabbed James Beard's Best Chef Southeast Award in 2009, after back-to-back nominations, and just six years after opening FIG, his first restaurant.

Not long after opening a second, completely extraordinary restaurant called The Ordinary (see page 143), Lata passed the FIG executive chef torch to his cultivated, hand-picked, protegee, Jason Stanhope. After a six year stint at FIG, where he started as a fish cook, the Topeka, Kansas native and Le Cordon Bleu (San Francisco) graduate quickly seized his own James Beard Best Chef Southeast Award for FIG in 2015.

Stanhope's clean, pure, exquisitely sourced culinary style is very compatible with the whole FIG mission. "There is a magic in restraint," says a reflective Stanhope, who considers his high school/college wrestling and football pursuits and sadly, the passing of his father at a young age, as the impetuses to what's become an amazing career in food. "I took this crazy gamble after Dad's death to go and gain traction (in my life) and attend Le Cordon Bleu. I completely fell in love with the sports-like aspect of team work, vision, being bigger than self," he says, alluding to a quote from football great Vince Lombardi. As for FIG, "everyone there coddles every step of the cooking and restaurant experience with every ounce of collective energy."

His classic, simple arugula salad, dotted with crispy shallots and aged cheese, is a perfect reflection of Stanhope's style. "We like to serve this salad on the larger side, a celebration of a few simple ingredients. All arugula is different so be sure to taste yours before seasoning and adjust accordingly—if it is heartier it might want more olive oil, if it's already spicy you might back down on the black pepper," he advises.

Stanhope includes a few more tips for making your salad the best it can be at home. "An easy alternative to frying your own shallots is to buy a bag of crispy shallots from an Asian market. But they are simple to make and will keep well in an airtight container at room temperature. We use a Pecorino Canestrato from Goat.Sheep.Cow (see page 202) but any hard, salty Italian cheese will work here. Using a micro-plane to grate the cheese yields a super fluffy pile that doesn't weigh down the salad. For this salad you can't really have enough crispy shallots or cheese."

CLASSIC ARUGULA SALAD

(SERVES 4–6)

3-4 cups canola oil, for frying

3 large shallots

½ cup cornstarch

16 ounces arugula, gently washed and dried thoroughly

6 tablespoons extra-virgin olive oil (we use domestic Arbequina)

1 tablespoon lemon juice

4–6 ounces Pecorino Canestrato, or any hard, salty Italian cheese such as Grana Padano or parmesan

1½ teaspoons coarse kosher or sea salt, or to taste

20 turns freshly cracked black pepper, or to taste

Fill a medium, heavy-bottomed pot about 2 inches deep with canola oil. (The oil will rise when you add the shallots so make sure the pot is less than half-way full). Using an insta-read or candy thermometer, heat oil to 275°F. Line a plate with paper towels and set aside.

Peel shallots and slice on a mandolin (or carefully slice) into rings about ⅛-inch thick. Toss with corn-starch to coat and shake off the excess. When the oil is ready, fry the shallots until golden and crispy, about 12–15 minutes. Stir gently, from time to time. Remove from oil with a slotted spoon and place on the paper towels to drain. Season generously with salt.

Place arugula in a large bowl and gently toss with olive oil until glossy. Season with salt and black pepper. Drizzle in the lemon juice and divide generously among 4-6 plates. Using a microplane, finely grate the Pecorino over each salad. Top with crispy shallots and season to taste with freshly cracked black pepper.

CHARLESTON SINGLE HOUSE

An architectural style designed to maximize cross-ventilating harbor breezes and privacy, the Charleston Single House, in both its classic and modified versions, can be spotted all around the peninsula and, increasingly, in new subdivisions beyond.

A true Charleston Single House runs perpendicular to the front property line, and the side (the gabled smaller end) actually faces the street. The house is only one room deep, with two rooms on each floor. Though a door is normally positioned facing the street, the formal entrance to the house is situated midway along the piazza, which typically shades all stories (usually two or three) of the house. Often the piazza overlooks a private garden. To honor Charlestonians' storied sense of propriety, the neighboring house on the garden side has just a few windows facing the garden, to encourage peak piazza privacy.

Cru Cafe on Pinckney Street

18 Pinckney Street, downtown
(843) 534-2434
crucafe.com
Executive Chef-Owner: John Zucker

The path to the world of food and restaurants was a winding one for John Zucker. Dreams of big-time baseball threw some curve balls in his early career, until an unlikely stint at a restaurant led John to his culinary wake-up call at the ripe old age of 27. After researching several culinary schools, John settled on Le Cordon Bleu in Paris, where he eventually graduated first in his class and with the full blessing of his mother. "Don't waste your time over there. Get it all done and do and learn all you can," John recalls her saying.

John took her advice and wasted no time getting his latter-day culinary career on track. He was surrounded by a posse of super talents at Spago in Los Angeles, where he continued to learn as a cook, and he eventually delved into restaurant consulting in both Atlanta and Charleston. He opened Cru Cafe in 2001, at a time when the Thai, Hispanic, and Asian ingredients and influences he espouses were relatively foreign here. "I said, hey, we're going to educate Charleston, and we did it. We were using habañeros and poblanos, and nobody knew what they were," explains John.

With perseverance and precision, John stood true to his commitment to "staying humble and keeping it fresh" in all menu items, including his starring salad player—Chinese Chicken Salad. It's a must-try at the warm, butter-yellow, modified Charleston Single House (see sidebar, page 40) at the corner of Pinckney Street and Motley Lane. Here, the clip-clop of passing horse-drawn carriages and seasonal wafts of wisteria fill the soul with a blissful sense of all being right in the world even when, just hours earlier, it seemed all wrong.

Chinese Chicken Salad

(SERVES 6–8)

For the roasted chicken:

1 cup garlic cloves

1 generous bunch fresh thyme, stemmed and coarsely chopped

1 tablespoon each salt and freshly ground black pepper, plus more to taste

1 large (3–4 pounds) chicken

For the dressing:

½ cup Colman's dry mustard

¾ cup peeled fresh ginger root cut into ½-inch chunks

¼ cup garlic cloves

½ cup soy sauce

¼ cup rice wine vinegar

¼ cup sesame oil

¼ cup red wine vinegar

2 cups peanut oil

¼ cup fresh-squeezed lime juice

¾ cup honey

Salt and freshly ground black pepper to taste

For the fried wontons:

3 cups peanut oil

15 prepared wonton wrappers (available at most grocery stores)

Salt to taste

For the salad:

3 cups julienned napa cabbage

½ cup peeled and julienned carrots

½ cup julienned daikon root

½ cup julienned red onion

½ cup julienned red bell pepper

½ cup julienned poblano peppers

Salt and freshly ground black pepper to taste

To prepare the chicken, preheat the oven to 425°F. In a bowl, mix together the garlic and the thyme. Season the mixture with the salt and freshly ground black pepper. Stuff the cavity of the chicken with the mixture. Season the chicken's exterior with additional salt and freshly ground black pepper. Place the chicken in a roasting pan or on a sheet pan and roast for 15 minutes. Reduce the heat to 375°F. Continue to cook the chicken until the juice runs clear when tipping the carcass, about 1 hour. Cool the chicken at room temperature. Once cooled, remove the skin and pick the chicken with your fingers or with a fork, pulling the meat into long strands. Discard the bones and skin. Set the picked chicken aside. (This can be done a day or two before preparing the salad.)

To prepare the dressing, combine the dry mustard, ginger, garlic, soy sauce, and rice wine vinegar in the bowl of a food processor. Blend until very smooth. With the motor still running, slowly drizzle in the sesame oil, the red wine vinegar, and the peanut oil. (If the dressing looks thick at this point, add

a little cold water to thin it.) Then gradually stream in the lime juice and honey. Taste and season with salt and pepper. Pour the dressing into a bowl and set aside.

To fry the wontons, heat the peanut oil in a large pot to 375°F. Stack the wontons, and, with a chef's knife, cut them into thin julienne strips. Place the strips in the hot oil all at once and fry until golden brown, about 2 minutes. With a strainer, carefully remove the wonton strips from the fryer and drain on paper towels. Drizzle with salt while the wontons are still hot.

To assemble the salad, combine the cabbage, carrots, daikon, red onion, red peppers, poblano peppers, picked chicken, dressing, and about one-third of the fried wontons in a large bowl. Season to taste with salt and pepper. Mound the salad in the center of individual plates. Top each mound with the remaining fried wontons. Serve immediately.

WHERE THE CHEFS SHOP

On Saturday mornings from early-April through mid-December, chefs and Charlestonians alike bow to the region's agri-bounty at the Charleston Farmers Market. A swirl of communal energy and good times fill the air, along with the enticing aroma of made-to-order crepes and frying mini doughnuts. Spot a chef or two inspecting collards or sampling a peach. Meanwhile, peruse the booths bursting with produce, jams, pickles, crafts, dog biscuits, and more. The market runs from 8:00 a.m. to 2:00 p.m. on Saturdays in season and is located on Marion Square between King and Meeting Streets, downtown. There are also smaller, more intimate and very popular farmers markets on nearby James Island, Johns Island, Daniel Island, and in Mount Pleasant.

The Glass Onion

1219 Savannah Highway, West Ashley
(843) 225-1717
ilovetheglassonion.com
Owner and Executive Chef: Chris Stewart

Southern influences from Chris Stewart's native Alabama extend all the way through New Orleans and the Lowcountry (two places where he's also spent a good amount of time), and fully unite to create broad, regional Southern cooking at The Glass Onion. Whether it's a grilled pimiento cheese po'boy on New Orleans bakery bread or Root Beer–Glazed Pork Belly with Grits and Greens, the theme here is high-quality nostalgic food at reasonable prices.

Though the food is Southern in style, its clarity is backed with experience in classical culinary technique and reverence for locally grown produce and hormone-free ingredients. Located on a busy highway in West Ashley, the restaurant has a breezy, sunny casualness punctuated with brown-paper-lined tables and a blackboard listing the day's seasonal specials.

Glass Onion fans line up for the restaurant's chicken salad, which is either served on a plate with greens (as in this recipe) or thickly spread between two slices of po'boy bread slathered with a layer of Duke's Mayonnaise (see sidebar page 18). The true goodness stems from the all-natural chicken and the patience of the brining and roasting process. At the restaurant, chicken salad plates and sandwiches are garnished with house-made bread-and-butter pickles and a deviled egg. It simply doesn't get any more satisfyingly Southern!

GLASS ONION ROASTED CHICKEN SALAD

(SERVES 4–6)

For the brine:

5 cups kosher salt

2 cups granulated sugar

1 cup red pepper flakes

3 tablespoons whole black peppercorns

2 tablespoons fennel seeds

3 bay leaves

1 bunch fresh thyme

1 bunch fresh rosemary

1 head of garlic, top trimmed off

2 whole chickens (1–2 pounds)

For the salad:

Salt and freshly ground black pepper to coat

1 cup finely diced celery

1 cup Duke's Mayonnaise

1 cup Zatarain's Creole Mustard

1 tablespoon Crystal Hot Sauce
2 teaspoons red wine vinegar
Salt and freshly ground black pepper to taste
4–6 leaves crisp lettuce for garnish
12 tomato slices for garnish

In a large pot or stockpot, combine all of the brine ingredients except the chicken and bring to a simmer over high heat. Simmer until the salt and sugar dissolve, about 5 minutes. Remove from the heat and cool to room temperature. Submerge the chickens in the brine. Refrigerate, covered, for at least 4 hours and up to 24 hours, turning occasionally.

To make the chicken salad, preheat the oven to 400°F. Rub both brined chickens generously with salt and freshly ground black pepper. Place back side down on a large roasting pan and cook on the middle rack of the oven for about 1 hour, or until a thermometer reads 165°F in the inner part of the chicken thighs. Allow to cool to room temperature. Pull the meat from the bones, discarding the bones, fat, and skin. Break the chicken into bite-size pieces or strands, either by pulling with a fork or by chopping coarsely. In a large bowl, combine the remaining ingredients (except the garnishes) with the chicken and stir well with a wooden spoon to combine. Taste and adjust salt and pepper as needed. Serve a generous scoop of the chicken salad on each plate, garnished with a large leaf of fresh lettuce and several tomato slices.

Leon's Fine Poultry & Oyster Shop

698 King Street, upper peninsula
(843) 531-6500
leonsoystershop.com
Executive Chef: Ben McLean

The epitome of Bohemian, New Orleans-inspired chic, Leon's is housed in a former body shop at the corner of King and I Streets in the increasingly restaurant-dense area of Upper King Streets. It's been the king of all things delicious since its opening in 2014, and is one of my absolute favorite restaurants in town, mostly because of its easy, whimsical style but especially for its always delicious food. Whether it's the made-to-order, extra spicy, crispy fried chicken, steaming hot from the fryer or fluffy, somewhere-between- a-donut-or-savory-corn-studded-hush puppy.

The eclectic, vintage 1950's décor is the perfect counter to the seasonally revolved menu, which showcases (as the name implies) chicken and oysters. Charbroiled oysters, slathered in just the right amount of butter, parsley, and lemon, are shucked at the bar, and 5 different raw varieties of the prized mollusks are showcased daily. Executive chef Ben McLean reports the restaurants sells up to 6,000 of them a week, and counting.

Much of the credit to the stellar consistency at the restaurant has to go to McLean, a Clemson, South Carolina native and former accounting student, his heart and soul eventually landed him at Cordon Bleu (Pittsburgh), a five-year stint at Peninsula Grill, as a line cook in Leon's early months, and now, as the king of the whole culinary shebang.

His substantive, yet still vegan, light and healthy whole grain spoon salad strikes the balance he strives for (and attains) in contrast to some of Leon's less figure-friendly dishes. "It's still filling

and approachable, and fills the niche as a substantive, healthy side for people that might also be drawn to the fried chicken," says McLean. He describes it, aptly, as "a mixed green salad you can get after as a side and eat with a spoon." I describe it as simply delicious and absolutely the ideal dish to create for a large, easy get together among friends.

WHOLE GRAIN "SPOON" SALAD

(SERVES 4–6)

For the barley:

1 cup pearled barley

Water to cover (see directions)

2 tablespoons kosher or sea salt

For the salad:

½ cup dried currants

½ cup finely chopped toasted pecans

¼ cup shaved or grated Parmesan cheese

½ cup diced red radish

¼ cup cherry tomatoes, halved

2 tablespoons finely chopped chives

2 tablespoons finely chopped parsley

2 tablespoons finely chopped celery leaves

Dress and season to taste with:

Extra virgin olive oil, fresh lemon juice, kosher or sea salt, freshly ground black pepper

Begin by preparing the barley. Rinse under cold water while agitating until the water runs clear and transfer to a 4-quart pot. Add enough cold water to cover the barley by about 3 times the volume. Add the salt, and set on medium-high heat. Once barley begins to boil, turn down to medium-low, and let simmer 10 minutes, stirring occasionally. When the barley is soft (yet still chewy), drain in a strainer small enough to hold all of the grains. Rinse barley under cold water to minimize starch and cool on a sheet pan.

While the barley is cooling, assemble and cut the remaining ingredients. Add currants, pecans, cheese, radish, and tomatoes to the barley in a large mixing bowl. Once these ingredients are mixed, add the herbs and celery leaves and begin to dress the salad with the oil and lemon juice. Finally, season to taste with salt and pepper. (Note: The barley can be prepared ahead and reserved separately. Combine the remaining salad ingredients within a few hours of service and serve at room temperature.)

Cafe Framboise

159 Market Street, downtown
843-414-7241
cafeframboise.com
Owners: Dominique and Florence Chantepie

"Passion" was the one-word response when I asked chef/owner Dominique Chantepie what he felt is the most important ingredient in good cooking. "I've been in this business 44 years and I still can't wait to get to work every day," says the Tours, France native who runs the cafe with his French wife Florence (front-of-the-house and business affairs). Cafe Framboise is the culmination of many years of culinary experience for the couple, who have worked in cities and kitchens all across France and the United States since their marriage in 1996.

They chose the name Cafe Framboise (which means 'raspberry' in French) because it sounded "fresh," and the freshness has stuck since its opening in 2015. Crepes, vol au vents, croissants so fresh and buttery you swear you're in Paris, quiches, soups, salads, and an entire, gorgeous arsenal of pastries from macaroons to Napoleans all made-in-house and overseen by Dominique in the cafe's petite, but passion-infused kitchen.

The adorably French cafe skips to an authentic and merry Gallic beat. Just walking in the door is an occasion to feel happy; the aromas so buttery, rich and intoxicating. The salad Niçoise is one of the biggest salad sellers at the cafe. As Dominique explains, it is often served as a composed, main course in France, but at the cafe, they serve individual portions tossed to order in their light, lemony, and addictive vinaigrette.

"We have changed the original recipe a bit to adapt to our tastes. Niçoise salads that are served in America are typically served with cooked green beans and potatoes," says Dominique. "In Nice, they would scream if you put potatoes in a Niçoise."

CAFE FRAMBOISE'S SALAD NIÇOISE

(SERVES 4–6)

For the vinaigrette:

⅓ cup fresh lemon juice

1 tablespoon French Dijon mustard

¾ cup extra virgin olive oil

Kosher or sea salt and freshly ground black pepper to taste

For the salad:

6 eggs, room temperature

3 tuna steaks (8 ounces each)

1 tablespoon olive oil (or substitute 2 cans of albacore tuna, well-drained)

2 heads butter lettuce, cut into bite-sized pieces

½ cup roasted red bell peppers (use either canned and drained or char your own fresh red bell pepper under the broiler or over an open flame, remove skin and seeds and coarsely chop)

3 ripe tomatoes, each cut into 6 or 8 wedges

¼ cup of Kalamata olives

¼ cup small anchovies if desired

1 tablespoon capers, if desired.

Kosher salt or sea salt to taste

To prepare the vinaigrette, shake together the lemon juice, olive oil and mustard in a covered canister until emulsified and well combined. (Or, in a small bowl, whisk together the lemon juice and mustard. Slowly stream in the olive oil, whisking all along to emulsify). Season to taste with salt and pepper. Reserve at room temperature (up to 1 day) until ready to use.

To prepare the salad, begin by boiling the eggs in boiling water for exactly 9 minutes. Remove, chill in ice water, peel, and cut into quarters, lengthwise. Set aside. Marinate tuna steaks in a little olive oil for an hour. Season both sides lightly with salt and pepper. Heat a large skillet over medium high heat, or place on a hot grill. Cook the steaks 2–3 minutes on each side until cooked through. Reserve warm and rest for 2 minutes.

Arrange bed of lettuce on a serving platter. Cut tuna into ½-inch thick slices. Mound the cut tuna (or substitute drained canned tuna) in the center of the lettuce. Arrange the tomatoes and bell pepper around the tuna. Arrange hard boiled eggs, olives, and anchovies (if using) in mounds on the lettuce bed. Drizzle everything with the vinaigrette. Sprinkle with capers if using. Season to taste with salt and pepper.

Serve immediately. Should be served slightly warm or at room temperature.

EDMUND'S OAST

1081 Morrison Drive, upper peninsula
(843) 727-1145
edmundsoast.com
Executive Chef: Bob Cook

Named after a British brewer who came to Charleston in the 1760's and used his brewing profits to help fund the Revolutionary War, Edmund and oast (a term for a kiln used to dry hops) respective spirits and crafts are alive and well at this bewitching brewery which is equally revered for its all-craft brewer beer selection and enticing eats.

The cavernous space attracts hoards to pair libations with the smoky fruits of the restaurant's extensive charcuterie program and executive chef Bob Cook's kitchen handiwork. The casual and hip nature of Edmund's Oast, as well as its easy access location and parking, attracts a large, diverse audience, thus creating a wide open tapestry upon which Cook works his magic.

"I have a deep respect for the [lives of the] animals that we choose to sustain our lives. To be wasteful and not use every little bit of its bounty would be disrespectful. So, we love to take it on our shoulders to be advocates of using of the less 'desirable' parts of the fish. In this case the texture of the cheeks and collar are a perfect texture to salt water poach and serve cold with an insanely flavorful dressing that is not only absorbed perfectly into the meat, but also plays great on all the different textures in the dish," explains Cook.

POACHED FISH COLLAR SALAD

(SERVES 6–8)

For the tamarind dressing:

¼ cup tamarind water

¼ cup fish sauce

¼ cup fresh lime juice

2 tablespoons palm sugar

1 tablespoon Thai chili paste

5 fresh Thai chilies, coarsely chopped

3 garlic cloves, peeled and coarsely chopped

Combine all ingredients in a blender or food processor and blend on low speed for approximately 1 minute. Reserve at room temperature for an hour or refrigerate, covered up to 2 days.

For the salad:

3 ounces poached white fish

3 poached large shrimp, halved

¼ cup fresh cilantro

½ cup shredded cabbage

¼ cup chopped spring onion

¼ cup fresh Thai basil

½ cup cherry tomatoes, halved

¼ cup shaved shallots or red onion

½ cup torn crispy lettuce (suggest romaine)

Combine all salad ingredients and mix. Add dressing and toss again. Taste and adjust seasoning as needed. Transfer to a large platter and serve cold.

Bull Street Gourmet and Market

120 King Street, downtown
(843) 722-6464
bullstreetgourmetandmarket.com
Executive Chef: Chris Evans

Executive chef Chris Evan's unique dialect and humble nature reveal his upstate New York origins, but there is an immense love of Charleston and good cooking engrained in his soul as well. Evans and his wife, Heather, who have backgrounds in private country club cooking and management, respectively, took a detour from Charleston for an attractive job in Florence, South Carolina. They found themselves very much missing Charleston. When he saw a post by a respected Charleston colleague for the job at Bull Street Gourmet and Market, he went for it.

Not only did the hours better suit his family lifestyle, but the deli nature jived with his cooking style. Situated on the cusp of Broad and Queen Streets in a largely residential area with a smattering of nearby realty and professional offices, and a significant amount of hungry pedestrian traffic, Bull Street Gourmet and Market is a popular breakfast and lunch destination.

"I like doing the simple things that I grew up with deli's serving sandwiches, salads, and soups. Except we try to do them in the best possible way," says Evans. His breakfast sandwich and egg salad sandwiches are two of Bull Street's daily best-sellers.

"This recipe is one of my favorites because it brings me back to my childhood when this would be in my lunch box two to three times a week. The only difference in this recipe than the one I remember my grandmother and mother using is the Duke's Mayonnaise. Growing up in the Northeast all salads were made with Hellman's. Being in South Carolina for so many years now, I have become a believer in Duke's," says Evans. (See sidebar, page 18)

Bull Street Egg Salad

(SERVES 4–6)

1 dozen eggs

½–¾ cup Duke's Mayonnaise (depends on how wet you like it)

1 tablespoon yellow mustard

2 ribs of celery, finely diced

½ of a small red onion, finely diced

Sea or kosher salt and freshly ground black pepper to taste

To hard boil eggs, gently set them in the bottom of a medium saucepan and cover generously with cold water over medium heat. After the water comes to a simmer, cook for exactly 12 minutes (Chef Evans sets a timer). Have ice water bath ready. After 12 minutes, gently lift the cooked eggs into the ice water and "shock" for 1–2 minutes to stop the cooking. Drain and refrigerate the eggs for 30 minutes (to facilitate peeling). Gently tap eggs and peel under slow stream of water at the sink. (Note: The eggs can be boiled and stored in a sealed container, refrigerated, for several days).

Grate the eggs on the large holes of a box grater over a large bowl. Add mayonnaise, mustard, celery, onion and stir gently to combine. Season to taste with salt and pepper. Serve on favorite bread or croissant. At Bull Street, the egg salad sandwich is served on a fresh croissant with Bibb lettuce, sliced tomatoes, sliced avocado and crisp smoked bacon.

SOUPS

In Charleston, women don't (heaven forbid) "sweat," nor do they "perspire." They "glow." But even though there is plenty of glowing going on come August, when temperatures hover around 100°F and the humidity flirts with 100 percent, Charlestonians love their soup. Hot or cold, winter or summer, it's a menu requisite. In her foreword to *Two Hundred Years of Charleston Cooking*, Elizabeth Verner Hamilton refers to "the Charleston habit of serving a properly balanced (afternoon) dinner of soup, rice and gravy, meat, two vegetables and a dessert at two or preferably 3 o'clock."

This tradition dates back to colonial times, but the city's modern chefs continue to put new twists on old favorites like she-crab soup. Grace Episcopal Church's time-worn recipe makes a return visit in this new edition, but newcomer Roadside Seafood's delectable frothy, smooth, creamy and sweet she-crab rendition is making a first time visit, along with Martha Lou's stewed lima beans and Crust's seasonally fresher-than-summer chilled summer corn soup by executive chef Dusty Chorvat.

Martha Lou's Kitchen

1068 Morrison Drive, upper peninsula
(843) 577-9583
marthalouskitchen.com
Owner/Partner and Executive Chef: Martha Lou Gadsen

It would be easy to discount the hot pink, cinder block bungalow, tattooed with nearly 40 years of eye-popping art that houses Martha Lou's Kitchen as just another roadside "dive." But, that would be a huge mistake. Martha Lou's Kitchen, run under the venerable hand of matriarch Martha Lou Gadsen, encapsulates the heart and soul, and earthy deliciousness of authentic Lowcountry cooking.

Chitterlings, fried pork chops, sweet corn bread, and made-to-order fried chicken that makes your belly rumble loudly in anticipation during the 20–30 minutes it takes to go from the order pad to your plate. Tattered, old pots and pans, vestiges of (mostly) cooking days past, clatter and clink along with Martha's cheerful, yet focused banter, as she works, alongside her daughter Debra in the restaurant's tiny, open kitchen. It's stupendous to contemplate the hugeness of the food that comes from wherein for decades.

Martha stays true to her original restaurant mission. Like the lima beans and everything else on her short, revolving menu, it's all about tradition. "When I opened, very few places served what I do, home-cooked food, doing my thing," she states both truthfully and proudly.

It's hard to pry an actual recipe out of a natural, time-tested cook, who measures nothing, tastes everything and hands the rest over to natural instinct. But, with a little effort, I was able to get her to share the secret to her celebrated stewed lima beans. Traditionally served over rice as a side, her version is delectable enough to eat as a stew, in a big bowl with a big spoon and an extra helping of eager.

STEWED LIMA BEANS

(SERVES 6–8)

1 pound dried lima beans
2 ham hocks or ham shanks
2 onions, coarsely chopped
1–2 tablespoons kosher or sea salt
2 teaspoons freshly ground black pepper
1–2 tablespoons granulated sugar
Water to cover

If you're cooking the stew on the same day, rinse the lima beans and pre-soak in hot water for 1 hour. If you're cooking the next day, rinse and pre-soak the lima beans in cold water, overnight. Either way, drain and rinse the beans thoroughly before proceeding.

Place the beans in a large pot with the ham hocks or ham shanks, onions, salt, pepper, and sugar ("It brings the flavor.") Cover generously (at least 4 inches of water covering the top) with cold water. Bring up to a boil, reduce to a simmer, and cook, uncovered, until the beans are very tender, 1–2 hours. "Simmer on down, until you have a thick gravy," says Martha. Remove the ham from the mixture and shave off the meat and return it to the pot, discarding bones, fat and cartilage.

Add additional water as needed to achieve desired "gravy" thickness, heat through, taste and adjust seasonings as needed. Serve very hot in a bowl as is, or over a bed of rice.

STEADY YUH HEAD

That's Gullah-speak for "think hard for the answer." The question, then, has to be, what exactly are Gullah and Geechee (also spelled "Geechi")? According to Charleston-based Gullah guru Alphonso Brown, both are names for a language and culture born in Africa. "Gullah derives from 'Gola' and Geechee comes from 'Kissi' (pronounced geezee). Both were tribes living in and around Sierra Leone in West Africa," explains the licensed Gullah tour guide and author of *A Guide to Gullah Charleston*. "More than 40 percent of Africans entering America came through Charleston harbor," says Brown. Many of the slaves who remained in the Lowcountry were from the rice-rich production areas of West Africa. Their skills were used to fuel the wealth of rice plantation owners here. The slaves' tolerance to malaria (which drove many wealthy whites away during peak season) and ability to congregate in slave-exclusive communities (especially in remote pockets of the barrier islands) allowed the slaves and their descendants to continue many of their cultural traditions and preserve their own language.

According to Brown, Gullah was a result of African Americans trying to learn English without being formally taught. "We were trying to speak good English. People always ask me how I learned to speak Gullah. I say, no, how did I get to learn English? English is my second language," Brown says. Cultural traditions, such as the art of weaving sweetgrass baskets, and gumbo (a derivative of an African word for "okra"), an okra stew, continue in the Lowcountry to this day.

Grace Episcopal Tea Room

98 Wentworth Street, downtown
(843) 723-4575
gracechurchcharleston.org

Wisteria and Confederate jasmine aside, nothing puts spring in Charleston's step more than the annual eleven-day-long rite of passage that is the Grace Episcopal Tea Room. Run in tandem with Spoleto Festival USA (the city's annual cultural and art festival), this "restaurant" is housed within the walls of a graceful historic church (established circa 1848) and the "chefs" are the ladies and gentlemen of the parish. Though ephemeral, it's an experience not to be missed. There are a few other tea rooms around town this time of year, but this one's the titan of sweet tea and all things Charlestonian.

The menu is composed of Lowcountry staples like okra soup, shrimp remoulade, and crab soup prepared with original recipes from church members' personal recipe files. Locals and visitors alike flock to share in their goodness while it lasts.

Expect to see a handsome gentleman host clad in full-on Charleston regalia: a seersucker suit, a dandy bow tie, a fresh magnolia boutonniere, and a broad-rimmed straw boater. He'll escort ladies to their tables as a piano man plays gentle tunes in the background. And just when you think it can't get any more deliciously Southern, you're reminded that all proceeds (hundreds of thousands of dollars since the tea room's 1992 debut) are designated for select area outreach programs.

After tweaking an old recipe from Everett's Restaurant (now defunct), the church ladies finally found the magic touch: Old Bay Seasoning. Serve the soup steaming hot and don't forget to pass a cruet of sherry along with it. That would be blasphemy.

CRAB SOUP

(SERVES 10)

1 pound fresh (or frozen) blue crab claw meat
5 tablespoons butter
1 cup finely chopped onion
1 cup finely chopped celery
1 quart whole milk
1 quart heavy cream
1 quart half-and-half
¼– ½ cup cornstarch
Generous dash of Worcestershire sauce
3 tablespoons sherry or to taste
1 tablespoon Old Bay Seasoning or to taste
Salt and freshly ground black pepper to taste

Pick over the crabmeat. Remove and discard all cartilage or shell bits. In a large pot, melt the butter over medium heat. Add the onion and celery, stirring to coat, and cook until softened and translucent, about 3 minutes. Add 3 cups of the milk, the cream and the half-and-half. Heat to just boiling, stirring often. Dissolve ¼ cup cornstarch plus 1–2 tablespoons for a thicker soup in the remaining 1 cup of milk and add to the soup, stirring well. Add the Worcestershire sauce, sherry, Old Bay Seasoning, and salt and pepper. Taste and adjust salt and pepper accordingly. When the soup is thickened (thickened enough to coat a spoon, about 20 minutes), add the crabmeat. Heat through over low heat. Thin with more heavy cream or half-and-half before serving if the soup is too thick as well as to "stretch for extra servings." Serve hot.

CHARLESTON'S VERY OWN TEA PARTY

Unlike their revolutionary compatriots in Boston, Charlestonians thought better of dumping tea into the Charleston harbor. Instead, they stored their overly taxed (without representation) tea in the cellar of the downtown Old Exchange Building where, a few years later, in 1776, South Carolina would sign her first Constitution and declare independence from Great Britain.

"The tea was later sold and used to fund the coffers of the newborn state. I think it's a wonderful story," says Denise LeCroy, a self-professed tea enthusiast and tea historian. A century later, Charleston would become home to what remains the only commercial tea plantation in North America, the Charleston Tea Plantation, currently situated on Wadmalaw Island, about 30 minutes from downtown. The tea plantation produces a black tea called American Classic that has officially been declared the hospitality beverage of the state of South Carolina. As if all that weren't enough to topple the crumpet cart, a twentieth-century visit to Charleston by author Owen Wister and a love-inspiring nibble of Lady Baltimore Cake here led him to write the story of *Lady Baltimore*, based on the woman who served him his first slice, says LeCroy.

Roadside Seafood

807 Folly Road, James Island
(843) 754-5890
roadsideseafood.com
Chef/Partner: Sean Mendes

Roadside Seafood began as a popular food truck canvassing James Island (about 10 minutes from downtown) in 2012, at the height of food truck popularity in Charleston. Very quickly, in 2014, it morphed into its own roadside, fish camp inspired version of a restaurant, touting its own, justifiably earned motto, "Yes, it's that 'bam' good."

The force behind the success is Charleston native chef/partner Sean Mendes. The Air Force baby (born in Guam) was mostly raised in Charleston by his native Charlestonian mother and Portuguese-American father, who hails from Rhode Island. The combined influences of his culinary gifted mother and grandmother and a penchant for the roadside sea shacks he visited as a kid, were the genesis of this wildly and worthily popular restaurant. "We went up to Rhode Island in the summers and I fell in love with these shacks serving the best fried seafood. I wanted to bring back that feeling of going to the beach with my parents and family and getting really great fried shrimp and local seafood," says Mendes.

The menu at ultra-casual and always packed Roadside Seafood is loaded with all of it--fried seafood plates, shrimp, oysters, "bam" shrimp tacos, and even more exotic offerings like frog legs, gator tail, and shark. The remoulade for dipping the shrimp is creamy, pink, sweet, tangy goodness and impossible to resist slathering on just about anything and the crispy, simple, and lightly dressed coleslaw recalls with breathless precision those I recall from fond memories of many New England roadside summer feasts.

But, the She-Crab soup is 100% Lowcountry. Prepared at Roadside with local blue crab, the crab weaves its essence, flavor and aroma into every sweet, frothy, creamy bite. It's an original from his grandmother's recipe box, what Mendes describes as "magic, timeless hard scribbled recipes perfected over time."

Use the freshest best-sourced crab you can find. Blue crab is what Mendes uses and recommends.

CHEF SEAN MENDES'S SHE-CRAB SOUP

(SERVES 6)

6 tablespoons unsweetened butter

¾ cup finely chopped celery

¾ cup finely chopped onion

½ cup all-purpose flour

2 cups clam juice

2 cups whole milk

1½ teaspoons fresh lemon juice

1 bay leaf

1½ teaspoons Worcestershire sauce

½ cup sherry

¼ teaspoon mace

¼ cup heavy cream

¼ cup crab roe

½ pound lump crab (preferably Lowcountry blue crab)

1 teaspoon kosher or sea salt

¼ teaspoon ground white pepper

Melt butter in a heavy bottom saucepan over medium heat without burning. Stir in the celery and onions, and cook for 1 minute. Sprinkle in flour, stir and cook for another minute. Add clam juice and whisk until smooth. Add milk and again whisk until smooth. Add remaining ingredients. Let simmer for 10 minutes, stirring occasionally. Remove the bay leaf. Once the soup has cooled down some, enjoy!

THE ORIGINS OF SHE-CRAB SOUP

The creation of she-crab soup is widely attributed to the butler and cook of early-twentieth-century Charleston mayor R. Goodwyn Rhett. Later to become a celebrated cook and restaurant chef, the former butler/cook named William Deas (whose direct descendant, celebrated Geechie Gullah chef Benjamin Dennis still resides and works here) was assigned a daunting task by the mayor's wife: to gussy up plain old crab. His trick was to add the orange- or pink-hued crab eggs that give the bisque or chowder its pretty, feminine pinkness and distinctive flavor.

The Restaurant at Middleton Place

Middleton Place
4300 Ashley River Road, West Ashley
(843) 556-6020
middletonplace.org
Executive Chef: Micah Garrison

Set on the hauntingly beautiful historic grounds of Middleton Plantation, the restaurant offers a feast for the senses as much as it does for the soul. The physical vestiges of what was one of Charleston's greatest rice plantations during the seventeenth and eighteenth centuries dot the sixty-acre landscape, lush with low-hanging live oaks and impeccable lawns and gardens. The visual stars here are a cascading staircase of verdant terraces leading down to the Ashley River and the rice beds that helped make the Middleton clan so sinfully wealthy. The Civil War (referred to more commonly in these parts as "the War of Northern Aggression") would put an end to all that and cause the destruction of the main house. The ruins and some outbuildings remain, but the showstoppers are the grounds and, of course, the restaurant.

It is housed in a small brick outbuilding that overlooks a graveyard where some of the Middleton slaves are buried and offers a sumptuous view of Rice Mill Pond. By day, an opportunity to dine is included with the price of admission to the museum. The restaurant's menu was originally created by recipe consultant and Middleton's longtime chef in residence, Edna Lewis. Executive chef Micah Garrison remains true to Edna's quintessentially Charleston recipes, including Huguenot Torte and shrimp and grits, particularly for the lunch menu. He dresses up dinner for the night crowd, issuing forth his insightful interpretations of Southern cooking.

In addition to the historic working environment, Micah draws inspiration from the organic garden on the grounds. For his okra and tomato gumbo, he advises using the freshest vegetables possible. This thick, fragrant soup is typically served over rice—a truly Charleston staple if ever there was one!

OKRA GUMBO

(SERVES 10)

2 tablespoons vegetable oil

5 stalks celery, cut into ¼-inch dice

2 large carrots, peeled and cut into ¼-inch dice

1 large onion, cut into ¼-inch dice

3 cups fresh corn, cut from the cob (or substitute frozen)

2½ cups fresh butter beans (or substitute frozen; see p. 64)

Salt to taste

2 cups tomato paste

2 teaspoons ground cumin

2 quarts high-quality vegetable stock

3 cups canned diced tomatoes with juice

8 cups fresh okra, cut into ½-inch-thick slices

2 tablespoons gumbo filé (see sidebar p. 64)

Freshly ground black pepper to taste

Heat a large soup pot over medium-high heat. Add the oil, celery, carrots, onion, corn, and butter beans with a pinch of salt. Cook, stirring, until the onion becomes translucent, about 5 minutes. Stir in the tomato paste and cumin, cooking briefly. Add the vegetable stock and diced tomatoes. Bring soup to a simmer. When the carrots are softened but still al dente, add the okra and gumbo filé. Simmer for about 15 minutes, or until the okra is softened and the gumbo has thickened. Season to taste with salt and pepper. Serve immediately, or better yet, serve the next day. Micah says it's better that way.

39 Rue De Jean

39 John Street, downtown
(843) 722-8881
39ruedejean.com
Chef de Cuisine: Jason Rambo

Beautifully honed to resemble an antique Parisian brasserie, 39 Rue de Jean (known to locals as "Rue") has universal appeal. Beefy house-ground burgers and steak frites comingle with delicate moules and hearty coq au vin to satisfy a kind of everyman hunger, yet Rue stays close to her Parisian roots. The young, attractive staff wear black and the waitresses look prêt-à-porter in their ruffled white aprons. Located in a former warehouse (built circa 1880), Rue has an authentic brasserie patina and glows with distressed mirrors, chocolate mahogany booths, old brick walls, and a bar imported from France.

A true neighborhood haunt in the happening Upper King Street area (the stretch of King between Calhoun and Spring Streets) of downtown, Rue has never wavered from its mostly Francophile mission. The Onion Soup Gratinée (along with the fluffiest, cheesiest, most delicious quiche in town), is a prime example. At the restaurant, it's prepared with equal parts house-made veal stock and chicken stock, swimming in a sea of sweet, caramelized onions kissed with sherry and topped with imported Gruyère brought to bubbling goodness in a hot oven.

Because it's easier to find high-quality prepared beef stock and beef bones to make your own stock, this recipe calls for beef stock instead of veal stock. Whatever you do, don't skimp on the principal components—a good stock (preferably homemade and salt-free), well-caramelized onions, and Gruyère cheese—and your Onion Soup Gratinée will taste just as authentically delicious as Rue's.

ONION SOUP GRATINÉE

(SERVES 8–10)

2 tablespoons olive oil
10 large yellow onions, thinly sliced
2 cups sodium-free chicken stock
2 cups sodium-free beef stock
2 tablespoons brandy
2 tablespoons sherry
Salt to taste
25 slices baguette, diagonally cut and toasted
25 slices Gruyère cheese

Heat a large soup pot over medium-high heat. Add the olive oil and heat. When the pan is hot, add the onions. Stirring constantly to prevent burning, reduce the heat to medium. Keep cooking and caramelizing the onions until they begin to brown and "all the natural sugars are out," 10–15 minutes. Remove from the heat and allow to cool for 10 minutes. Add the chicken stock and beef stock and bring the mixture to a boil over high heat. Add the brandy and sherry. Season to taste with salt.

To serve, preheat the oven to 400°F. Ladle the hot soup into deep ovenproof soup bowls (or bistro bowls), leaving room for the toast and cheese. Top each with 2-3 toast points and 2-3 slices Gruyère cheese. Bake the soup in the bowls for 8–10 minutes or until the cheese is brown and bubbly. Serve immediately.

MYSTERY INGREDIENTS: BUTTER BEANS AND GUMBO FILÉ

Unless you're from the South, butter beans and gumbo filé may be entirely new to you. Embrace both! Butter Bean is the perfect name for the pale green (or sometimes speckled) legume that thrives during Charleston's long, hot summer months. Its smooth, even flavor and soft, yielding flesh recalls creamery-fresh butter. The beans are used in everything from soups to salads. If you have trouble finding them, the slightly larger lima bean will make a fine substitute. Gumbo filé hails from Cajun country and is made of ground sassafras leaves. It is used here to both season and thicken the soup. Look for it in Cajun specialty stores or online.

Crust Wood Fired Pizza

1956 Maybank Highway, James Island, (843)762-5500
1097 N. Main Street, Summerville (843) 285-8819
crustwoodfirepizza.com

Executive Chef: Dusty Chorvat

Don't let his shy and unassuming demeanor fool you. Dusty Chorvat is oozing with talent and passion for cooking, especially anything that abides by his religious-like devotion to cooking seasonally with impeccably sourced local ingredients. The self-taught chef and former music student of The Art Institute of Atlanta dappled his genius all over town working either as a consultant or chef in many of the excellent restaurants in this book, including EVO, The Glass Onion and Monza.

His latest undertaking and the one most closely aligned with his pristine cooking style is at Crust, where he serves as executive chef at the James Island location and consultant at the newer location in Summerville. Both locations feature a wood fire oven operating at a scorching 900°F, fueled by kiln dried oak. It's that kind of heat that puts the delightful charred bubbles on Chorvat's perfectly chewy, dense, flavor-packed pizzas—all decorated with exclusively local produce and house-made cheeses and sausage.

Though pizza is in the name, it's by no means the only thing to order at sublime Crust. Chorvat's salads practically glisten with freshness and are lusciously and deftly dressed with house-made buttermilk and blue cheese or sassy vinaigrettes.

Daily special menus reflect the season, from whence this creamy, naturally sweet corn soup was born. Sunny and bright, it both tastes and looks like summer. Use the freshest corn you can find, as it really is the principle ingredient in this soup. In typical Chorvat style, he lets the main ingredient shine, completely unfettered by pretense or complication, not unlike the remarkably talented chef himself.

Chilled Summer Corn Soup

(SERVES 4-6)

For broth:

4 reserved corn cobs (from cobs shucked for soup ingredients)

4 cups water

1 bay leaf

1 teaspoon kosher or sea salt

1 approximately 2-inch by 2-inch rind of Grana Padano or Parmesan cheese rind

For the soup:

4 ears of corn (yellow preferred for color) shucked, or about 4 cups of kernels. Reserve cobs for broth.

¼ cup diced red onion

1 teaspoon minced garlic

2 tablespoons extra virgin olive oil

½ teaspoon kosher or sea salt

¼ teaspoon freshly ground black pepper

1 cup roughly chopped good quality Tuscan bread

For the garnish:

4 grape tomatoes, thinly sliced

2 slices cooked bacon, coarsely chopped

1 tablespoon thinly sliced chives

Extra virgin olive oil, to drizzle

Prepare the broth. Place corn cobs, water, bay leaf, salt and cheese rind in a 4-quart pot. Bring to a boil over high, reduce to a simmer and cook with lid on for 10 minutes. Meanwhile, in a large, 8-inch sauté pan, sauté the corn kernels, red onion, garlic, olive oil and salt and pepper over medium heat until garlic is fragrant and slightly browned, about 5 minutes. Add chopped bread. Toss and set aside.

Strain broth into a separate container & discard solids. Now put the corn mixture into the 4-quart pot and pour broth over it. Bring back to a boil and simmer, covered, for 10 minutes to soften bread & infuse flavors. Place soup in blender & purée until smooth & silky. Chill (at least several hours or overnight) and serve cold, in individual bowls with an artful drizzle of the garnish on top of each.

Circa 1886

149 Wentworth Street, downtown
(843)853-7828
circa1886.com
Executive Chef: Marc Collins

The year 1886 was a rough one for Charleston. With the town still reeling from the devastating financial and structural ruin of the Civil War, an earthquake had the audacity to roll through, killing an estimated sixty people and sending many a building tumbling down. Not so for the stalwart mansion at 149 Wentworth Street (now a AAA Five Diamond hotel known as the Wentworth Mansion). The home of a wealthy sulfur magnate at a time when nearly everyone else in Charleston was poor, it was constructed the same year as the earthquake. It's rumored, according to executive chef Marc Collins, that the cupola of the imposing brick structure was built expressly so the owner could "look down" on all of Charleston, but it was more likely a spotting post for the fire department. Either way, the owner probably wasn't a terribly popular guy among the "too poor to paint, too proud to whitewash" set.

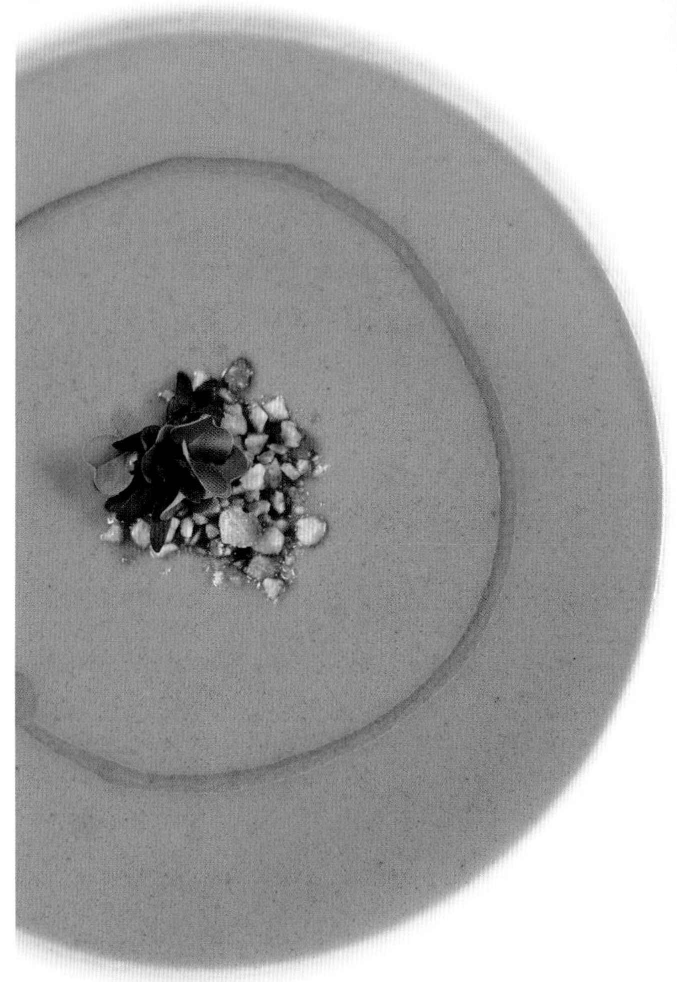

Circa 1886 is housed in the mansion's original carriage house. Marc keeps the restaurant's menu and mood universe small and uniquely Charleston. "When I sit down to write recipes, I write with Charleston's influences from 200 years ago, when it was such a large port city. The spice trade, slavery, French Huguenot, Caribbean flavors—they're all melded into the menu," he explains. At Circa 1886, this soup is frequently served as an amuse-bouche to jump-start lucky guests' dinners.

PEANUT SOUP

(SERVES 6–8)

1 tablespoon olive oil or vegetable oil

1 cup diced celery

1 cup diced onion

1 cup raw or dry-roasted peanuts, plus finely chopped peanuts for garnish (optional)

3 tablespoons soy sauce

3 tablespoons rice wine vinegar

1 tablespoon Tabasco sauce

2 quarts chicken stock

1 cup peanut butter

Salt to taste

Chili oil for garnish (optional)

Heat the olive oil in a soup pot over medium heat. Add the celery and onion and stir. Cook gently until translucent, 3–5 minutes. Add the peanuts and cook for 4 minutes, stirring frequently. Add the soy sauce, vinegar, Tabasco sauce, and stock. Continue simmering until the peanuts are soft, about 30 minutes. Strain the soup to separate the liquids from the solids, reserving both separately. Puree the vegetable and peanut solids in a blender or food processor, adding just enough liquid to cover the puree. Slowly add the rest of the liquid while pureeing.

Return the soup to the stove and bring to a simmer. Whisk in the peanut butter, heat through, adjust salt as needed, and serve. Garnish with a sprinkle of finely chopped peanuts or a drop or two of chili oil, if desired.

THE OLD CITY MARKET

Between Meeting and East Bay Streets in the heart of downtown is a string of our open-air brick buildings that bulge with incongruous bedfellows—kitschy curios, packaged foodstuffs, and beautiful sweetgrass baskets. Open seven days a week and surrounded by several carriage tour companies, restaurants, and shops, it's a frequent tourist haunt. For that reason, along with a dearth of easy parking, many locals avoid the area. Yet everyone should go—at least once. There are many (often negotiable) roses to be found among the useless thorns, and the hustle and bustle is inspiring when the mood is right. The main building of the market is called Market Hall. Built in 1841, it is now home to the Daughters of the Confederacy Museum. In the old days, the market area was a vending area for local seafood, meats, vegetables, and fruits. It has been hotly debated whether it should return to its original purpose and be closed off to cars in an effort to lure more regular local traffic.

Amen Street Fish & Raw Bar

205 East Bay Street, downtown
(843) 853-8600
amenstreet.com
Executive Chef: Garrett Priester

Located a few blocks from The Old City Market, one of the first things you'll likely notice about this comely restaurant-meets-oyster bar are the stunning oyster chandeliers, unless the busy oyster shuckers at the bar don't catch your eye first.

Amen's executive chef and Beaufort, South Carolina native, prays to the gods of fresh and local fish at this relaxed and cosmopolitan restaurant. The menu features up to 70 or 80 oyster varieties on any given day, and several varieties of local fish with assorted sauces and sides. "Whatever it is we treat it well and simply, season and cook it," the minimalist and freshness-driven chef explains.

Though Priester, a Culinary Institute of Charleston graduate, loves cooking year round, it's March and the kick-off of the local seafood season that really puts a spring in his step. "We have local captains from Shem Creek, Murrell's Inlet and other local waters bringing it in every day. It's amazing!"

Whether you're in the mood for raw oysters, Amen Street's "famous" and absolutely fun and delicious shrimp corndogs, herb-seared or blackened striped bass or flounder (and several other local fish choices), you'll be in fine celestial glory here.

Though technically a side, the restaurant's creamed corn is the stuff of dreams and could probably also be considered a kind of stew or even a warm salad, so I'm jockeying it between the soup and salad chapters, because it's not-to-be missed. Priester says his wife always orders it, that and the fried shrimp. Do not try and make this into a more liquid soup, advises Priester, because unless finely pureed with the addition of more stock or water, it will break due to the cream cheese. I promise you, it is perfect as is.

AMEN ST. CREAM CORN

(SERVES 6–8)

1½ cups cream cheese

4 cups heavy cream (40% cream)

1 tablespoon kosher or sea salt

1 teaspoon freshly ground black pepper

8 cups (about 10 large ears) freshly shucked and cut off the cob yellow sweet corn, silk removed and discarded

Warm cream cheese and cream over medium high heat in a large saucepan, stirring often to avoid scorching. Once the cream cheese has melted into heavy cream, add salt and pepper and stir to combine evenly. Add corn and, stirring, and reduce to low heat. Cook on low for 5 minutes, continuing to stir constantly. Serve immediately

SHUCKING AROUND

Chef Garrett Priester not only grew up in Beaufort, a famous fishing and shrimping town about 100 miles south of Charleston, but he learned fishing and oysters from the best. His grandfather was an engineer-turned-shrimper and operated two shrimp boats. I asked for any tips he would be willing to share about shucking oysters, something I'm admittedly not very good at and something I've observed most other people are not, either.

Here's his expert advice:

"Every oyster is a little bit different. But they've all got a hinge that needs to be popped with the tip of the oyster knife. Insert the tip into the hinge, give a slight rotation of your wrist, firmly gripping the oyster, and that should pop the hinge. Run the flat side of the knife along the shell to release the shell, and then cut the other foot (attaching the oyster to the shell), to release the oyster meat. Flip the oyster inside the cup (of the shell) to see both sides and remove any debris that may have broken off from the shell."

Sandwiches

John Montagu, the 4th Earl of Sandwich, for whom the sandwich is thought to have been named, would surely be surprised by the diversity and popularity his favorite bread-enveloped snack has achieved since the eighteenth century. So much more than something to wrap up cold meats or keep hands free while eating, sandwiches these days are round-the-clock hunger-stomping staples.

Coincidentally, "Montagu" is the big name in Charleston. It (and a variation on the theme) is the name of two major thoroughfares here, a testament to Charleston's Huguenot past and present.

One might predict a preponderance of dainty crustless cocktail-party shrimp, egg salad, and chicken salad sandwiches on Charleston's restaurant menus, but the opposite is true. Gargantuan portions fit for the famished, and gourmet touches fit for a king (let alone an earl) abound. Jack's Cosmic Dogs goes galactic with hot dogs topped with crunchy blue cheese slaw and slathered with sweet potato mustard. Poe's Tavern takes burgers to eerily delicious heights with its "Sleeper" burger of 100 percent certified Angus chuck decked out with buffalo shrimp and roasted garlic blue cheese. Or, go double-duty with Husk's (quite literally) famous double cheeseburger; Minero's benne salsa blessed mula quesadilla with toasted veggies; and Boxcar Betty's sizzling, fresh-from-the-fryer blue cheese sauce, tomato, bibb and warm Buffalo sauce drenched fried chicken sandwich.

Don't waste any time: grab your appetite and a hefty stack of napkins and dig right in. There's no doubt the celebrated earl would if he could.

Poe's Tavern

2210 Middle Street, Sullivan's Island
(843) 883-0083
poestavern.com
Kitchen Manager: Chris Schultz

Telltale clues of Edgar Allan Poe's life and works lurk in the many nooks of this beach bungalow, situated on the island where Poe was stationed as a U.S. Army soldier in 1827 and where he penned "The Gold Bug." Black silhouettes of Poe's tragic countenance and several ravens set a dark mood that is all at once lightened by the hipster, relaxed beach groove at Poe's.

The central bamboo-topped bar is open and invites sea breezes and easy conversations, rendering Poe's very much a popular watering hole. But folks come to Poe's just as much for the restaurant's epic burgers and fish tacos as its beer. All the burgers are cleverly named for Poe stories (Pit & Pendulum, Black Cat, and, of course, Gold-Bug) and are prepared with certified Angus chuck, ground in-house and cooked to order. Non-beef eaters can substitute a substantial, 6-ounce, skinless grilled chicken breast for any of the burger options.

The Sleeper, a 6-ounce burger topped with roasted garlic blue cheese and fried buffalo shrimp, was a special that was so revered it earned a permanent spot on Poe's menu.

THE SLEEPER

(SERVES 6)

For the garlic blue cheese sauce:

¼ cup garlic cloves (about 8 cloves)

1 tablespoon olive oil

1 pound blue cheese, coarsely crumbled

¾ cup mayonnaise

Kosher or sea salt and freshly ground black pepper to taste

For the burgers:

2 pounds, 4 ounces freshly ground certified Angus choice chuck beef (ask your butcher to grind the beef to your specifications when you purchase it)

Kosher or sea salt and freshly ground pepper to taste

For the buffalo fried shrimp:

2 cups milk

1 egg

Salt and freshly ground black pepper to taste

2 cups all-purpose flour

1 tablespoon Old Bay Seasoning

30–36 medium shrimp, peeled and deveined, tails removed

3 cups peanut oil

1 cup Texas Pete Mild Chicken Wing Sauce (or Hot Chicken Wing Sauce, if desired)

To serve:

6 high-quality hamburger buns (Poe's are made by a local bakery)

POE'S
TAVERN

Prepare the garlic blue cheese sauce up to 3 days in advance. Preheat the oven to 375°F. Line up the garlic cloves on a small roasting pan and drizzle with olive oil. Cover tightly with aluminum foil. Roast until golden brown, about 30 minutes. Set aside to cool. When cooled, blend garlic in the bowl of a food processor until smooth. Transfer the garlic puree to a medium bowl and combine, stirring gently, with the blue cheese, mayonnaise, and salt and pepper to taste. Cover and refrigerate until ready to use.

Meanwhile, form the hamburger into six 6-ounce patties. Season the exteriors lightly with salt and pepper. Cover with plastic wrap and refrigerate up to 12 hours before cooking.

To prepare the fried shrimp, combine the milk, egg, and salt and pepper to taste in a shallow bowl, mixing well with a fork. Separately, combine the flour, Old Bay Seasoning, and salt and pepper to taste in a second shallow bowl, mixing well with a fork.

To bread the shrimp, first dip in the flour mixture, tapping off any excess, then dip in the milk and egg mixture, then finish by dipping in the flour mixture again. Be sure to tap off any excess flour. Set shrimp aside.

Just before serving, heat the peanut oil in a medium saucepan over medium heat until it reaches 325°F to 350°F. In the meantime, cook the burgers on a grill or in a large sauté pan over medium or medium-high heat to desired doneness. Remove and set aside, keeping warm. When the oil is hot, fry the shrimp in batches until they are golden brown, about 2 minutes. Remove with a slotted spoon and drain over paper towels. When cool enough to handle, toss the shrimp with the hot sauce in a medium bowl.

To serve, place each burger on a bun and top with about ¼ cup of the garlic blue cheese sauce. Top with five or six warm Buffalo Shrimp. Serve immediately and pass the napkins!

LITTLE BIG SHRIMP

Shrimp are to the Lowcountry what crawfish are to Louisiana. The salt water that wraps its way around the coastal plain and weaves into the region's complex network of marshes and tributaries provides a nurturing environment for shrimp to spawn and grow before they're harvested. When that happens (generally the season runs from May or June until the first frost in December or January), shrimp of all sizes show up boiled, fried, stewed, and baked; in delicate dips, soups, salads, casseroles, deviled eggs, and omelets; and, of course, on top of grits.

Unlike shrimp "from off" (as Charlestonians refer to all things not from here), local shrimp are smaller, sweeter, and distinctive. Once you've tasted them, you'll never go back. In the warmer months, the smaller brown shrimp are running. Look for the slightly larger white shrimp, which are arguably sweeter and definitely meatier, in fall and winter.

Jack's Cosmic Dogs

2805 Highway 17 North, Mount Pleasant
(843) 884-7677
jackscosmicdogs.com
Owner: "Big Dog" Jack Hurley

After graduating from the College of William & Mary with a business degree in 1972, Jack Hurley decided he was "done being told what to do." So he put together his own bucket list and hitch-hiked, skied, took a train across the Rockies, met his wife, and otherwise played until he turned 27. That year, the maverick who calls himself "Big Dog" discovered his trade and opened his first restaurant in Burlington, Vermont. Many moons and several successful restaurants and businesses later, the Big Dog still barks with joy as the top dog at Jack's Cosmic Dogs, a hip hot dog joint that combines Jack's love for all things quirky and cosmic and wraps it all up in an oversized Pepperidge Farm bun.

A Flash Gordonesque model rocket, moon pies, cream sodas, a 1950s-style cooler, and a red Sunbeam white bread sign give Jack's a comforting blast-from-the-past feel with a new age twist. Throw in 98 percent beef (the remaining 2 percent is pork) Boar's Head dogs and a smattering of original condiments from Jack's repertoire, and it's no surprise that Jack's got kids of all ages bow-wowing for more.

Tangy blue cheese slaw and Jack's jarred sweet potato mustard (available for purchase on his website) dress up Jack's signature cosmic dog. The sweet heat from the mustard is the perfect foil for the mellow bite of blue cheese and the crunch of the slaw and is part of what makes this dog so hot-diggedy-dog delicious. Meanwhile, there's no reason for vegetarians to skip this party: the "Vegaroid" Dog features Morningstar tofu dogs slathered with yellow mustard, ketchup, and onions.

Jack's Cosmic Dog

(SERVES 6)

For the blue cheese slaw:

1 small head green cabbage, finely sliced
¼ small head red cabbage, finely sliced
1 carrot, peeled and finely sliced
1 cup sour cream
1 cup mayonnaise
1½ teaspoons garlic powder
½ teaspoon dried oregano
½ teaspoon onion powder
½ cup crumbled high-quality blue cheese
Kosher or sea salt and freshly ground black pepper to taste

For the hot dogs:

6 Boar's Head hot dogs (Jack also recommends Hebrew National hot dogs)
6 Pepperidge Farm oversized hot dog buns
¼ cup Jack's Sweet Potato Mustard

Up to 2 hours before serving, combine all of the slaw ingredients in a large bowl, stirring well to combine. Taste and adjust seasoning as needed. Cover and reserve at room temperature.

Steam or grill the hot dogs according to package directions. To assemble the hot dogs, spread a generous tablespoon of Jack's Sweet Potato Mustard on both sides of the inside of each bun. Top the mustard-swathed buns with the warm hot dogs and about ¼ cup of the slaw. Serve immediately. At Jack's, the dogs come with a cone of sweet potato French fries.

Nothing
drinking if you had not made them a pleasure as well as

Five Loaves Cafe

43 Cannon Street, downtown, (843) 937-4303
1055 Johnnie Dodds Boulevard, Suite 50, Mount Pleasant, (843) 849-1043
214 N. Cedar Street, Summerville, (843) 804-9410
fiveloavescafe.com
Partners/Owners: Casey Glowacki and Joe Fischbein
Corporate Chef: Jason Ulak

Not even divorce, a beloved dog's death, jury duty, and excruciating back pain could deter tenacious chef-turned-businessman Casey Glowacki from achieving his dream and opening his first restaurant, Five Loaves Cafe. Unbelievably, all those nasty things converged during the restaurant's early days, back in 2003. Not only did the restaurant survive, it thrives as the "great little soup and sandwich shop" he and his business partner, Joe Fischbein, envisioned. Unlike the original plan, however, demand for Five Loaves was so hot that the menu was expanded to include dinner and, later, a second location in Mount Pleasant, and a third, most recently in Summerville.

Five Loaves teems with bohemian energy and garden-fresh goodness. Sandwiches are served on six mix-and-match varieties of bread made daily at a local bakery. Long-time Charleston-based chef, Jason Ulak, now oversees the three kitchens as corporate chef. Robin-egg blue benches make for comfortable perches, and quotations from artists and authors inlaid in each table make for witty reading at the signature downtown location, while savoring the many vegetarian, gluten-free and other delights from the kitchen(s).

This yummy vegetarian sandwich, one of many vegetarian offerings at the restaurants, is a rendition of a recipe that Casey prepared at a deli and gourmet market he once worked at in Telluride, Colorado. It tastes just as good in Charleston. Though formerly a stalwart on the menu, these days it takes turns as a sandwich special.

ROASTED PORTOBELLO SANDWICH WITH SWEET ONION, ROASTED RED PEPPER, AND PARMESAN SPINACH SPREAD

(SERVES 6)

For the mushrooms:

6 whole portobello mushrooms, stems removed
4 tablespoons chopped garlic
2 tablespoons olive oil
Salt and freshly ground black pepper to taste

For the sweet onions:

1 tablespoon olive oil
1 onion, finely sliced
Salt and freshly ground black pepper to taste

For the roasted red peppers:

2 red bell peppers

For the Parmesan spinach spread:

1 cup grated sharp cheddar cheese
2 cups grated Parmesan cheese
¼ cup mayonnaise
2 cups fresh spinach, tough stems removed
Salt and freshly ground black pepper to taste

For the sandwiches:

12 thick slices high-quality whole-grain bread (or substitute preferred bread type)

1 large tomato, thinly sliced

1½ cups fresh mesclun

To prepare the mushrooms, preheat the oven to 375°F. Gently rub the garlic into the rib-side (interior) of the mushroom caps. Lay caps rib-side up on a sheet pan and drizzle with olive oil, salt, and pepper. Roast for 12 minutes. Set aside to cool.

Meanwhile, prepare the onions. Heat the olive oil over medium heat in a medium sauté pan. Add the onion, season with salt and pepper, and cook until the onions take on a golden color and are very soft, about 12 minutes. Set aside.

Roast the peppers over an open gas flame on the stovetop, turning occasionally to blacken the entire surface of each pepper. (The peppers can also be roasted under the broiler or purchased prepared.) Rinse the roasted peppers under a steady stream of cold water, removing the blackened skin, ribs, and seeds. Chop the roasted pepper into coarse strips and set aside.

Prepare the Parmesan spinach spread by combining the cheddar, Parmesan, mayonnaise, fresh spinach, and salt and pepper in the bowl of a food processor. Blend until chunky-smooth. Adjust seasoning as needed.

To assemble the sandwiches, line up the bread slices on your working surface. Spread one side of each slice with Parmesan spinach spread. Top six of the slices with about ¼ cup of mesclun and 2 tomato slices. Top with 1 roasted portobello cap and a portion of the sweet onions and roasted pepper. Top with the remaining slices of bread. Serve immediately.

Gaulart & Maliclet

98 Broad Street, downtown
(843) 577-9797
fastandfrench.org
Manager/Co-Owner: Jennifer Bryant
Co-Owner: Lawrence Mitchell

You won't be served a Coca-Cola or any kind of soft drink to wash down your chien chaud at this endearing French cafe, more commonly referred to as Fast & French. That's because Parisian native and former owner Gwylene Gallimard doesn't believe in clobbering good food with the cloying sweetness of Coke. "We serve wine to balance the food. It should not overpower the food, but complement it," she says. Water, micro-brewed beers, and sweet tea are alternative choices to pair with the cafe's myriad soup and sandwich lunch combinations and très French dinner menu, composed of bouillabaisse, house-made fondue, escargot, and couscous.

Jean-Marie Mauclet, Gwylene's partner in life and business, grew up in his grandfather's cafe and his mother's kitchen in northern France and was the original creative genius behind nearly all of the tantalizingly French, yet homey recipes that have been dished out here for a quarter of a century. Folks return time and again for the relaxed Francophile environs and the bohemian buzz created by the scent of rich coffee and the quiet banter of the mostly black-clad guests.

Gwylene and Jean-Marie sold the restaurant in 2011 to pursue their visual artistry dreams and handed over the restaurant reigns to long-term employees Jennifer Bryant and Lawrence Mitchell. Other than that, little else has changed at the restaurant, which remains utterly true to its Francophile roots, including the menu and this spunky sandwich that is served warm and made to order. Make a big batch of the tapenade—this recipe makes enough for about twenty sandwiches—and save the leftovers to serve as an appetizer with cheese and wine. The tapenade will store for several days in the refrigerator. Bon appétit!

Sandwich Provençale

(MAKES 1 SANDWICH)

For the tapenade:

2½ cups pitted olives (green or black niçoise), coarsely chopped

1¼ cups extra-virgin olive oil

2½ green bell peppers, seeded and cut into quarters

2 large tomatoes, cored and coarsely chopped

1 medium zucchini, peeled and coarsely chopped

½ cup coarsely chopped fresh parsley

1 tablespoon fresh-squeezed lemon juice, or to taste

6 cloves fresh garlic, coarsely chopped

1 tablespoon freshly ground black pepper

Kosher or sea salt to taste

For the sandwich:

¼ of a high-quality fresh baguette, sliced lengthwise

bodum
PEBO
BISTRO

1 ounce fresh goat cheese

2 slices fresh tomato

2 teaspoons chopped fresh basil

Taste the olives you're using for the tapenade before you get started. If they're extra salty, rinse them to remove excess salt, and keep their salt content in mind as you're seasoning. To prepare the tapenade, combine all the tapenade ingredients in the bowl of a food processor and pulse together until the consistency is medium-fine. You want the pieces to be about one-quarter the size of a pea. Taste and adjust seasoning as necessary. (The tapenade can be prepared several days in advance and stored in the refrigerator. For the best flavor, use the tapenade at room temperature.)

To assemble the sandwich, preheat the broiler or a toaster oven to high. Spread one half of the sliced baguette with goat cheese. Place both halves of the baguette, cut side up, under the broiler or in the toaster oven and toast until the bread is crisp and golden and the cheese has softened. Evenly spread the tapenade on the bare half of the sandwich and top this with the tomato slices. Sprinkle the goat cheese half with the fresh basil. Serve immediately, either open-faced or closed.

STOP

BOXCAR BETTY'S

1922 Savannah Highway, West Ashley, (843) 225-7470
114 Holiday Drive, Summerville, (843) 225-9843
boxcarbetty.com
Co-Owners: Ian MacBryde and Roth Scott

The innovative and prescient Boxcar Betty's ownership team hatched their plot to create way-better-than-fast-food fried chicken sandwiches when they were working the front of the house together at Magnolias (page 30). Because, "no one else was doing it," explains Roth Scott. They spotted the void before anyone else in town, unless you count southern fried chicken sandwich God Chick-fil-A, located just a few doors down. If not heresy itself, this was definitely a gutsy move. But it worked. Southern natives (MacBryde hails from North Carolina and Scott from Kentucky), they put their heads together to come up with a winning formula that was so hot, it soon carried over to opening a second location in Summerville.

All of the chicken here is natural, cage-free, antibiotic-free and locally sourced. That's not the only difference. According to Roth, it's all in the (largely secret brine), and of course hot, fresh, regularly changed canola oil and house-made condiments and sauces. They all reach a crescendo in the best-selling Buffalo fried chicken sandwich with pungent, creamy blue cheese sauce and garden fresh tomato slices and crunchy, buttery Bibb lettuce. Cool contrasts with the hot, creamy complements the vinegar pluck, and crunch melts into the soft, white bun to make the perfect sandwich.

Housed in a small yet easily accessed space that resembles an actual train boxcar (because the original plan was to start the restaurant near the train station in North Charleston), it feels slightly country and very friendly eating here. And the chicken, well, it goes way beyond finger licking good. Locals and tourists alike clamber aboard for the hot-from-the-fryer deliciousness at Boxcar Betty's.

BOXCAR'S BUFFALO, BLUE CHEESE SAUCE, TOMATO AND BIBB LETTUCE FRIED CHICKEN SANDWICH

(MAKES 4 SANDWICHES/SERVINGS)

For the fried chicken:

1 package commercial poultry brine (see sidebar, page 92)

4 6-ounce skinless chicken breasts

2 cups buttermilk

½ cup Dijon mustard

4 cups all-purpose white flour

¼ cup garlic powder

¼ cup onion powder

¼ cup black pepper

¼ cup kosher or sea salt

2 cups canola oil for frying

4 soft potato rolls (suggest Pane Di Vita potato sandwich rolls, Martin's potato sandwich rolls, or an alternate brand of potato sandwich rolls)

4 tablespoons unsalted butter for toasting rolls

IT'S IN THE BRINE, BOY

Brining is a popular method for tenderizing and preserving moisture in meat, especially white poultry meat, though there is a brine for everything it seems, from pork to salmon. It's usually a combination of water (or another liquid), salt, sugar and seasonings. Although the actual recipe at Boxcar Betty's is secret, Roth did share the basic brine ratio of 1 gallon water to ⅓ cup each salt and sugar. You'll want to play with some basic seasoning to come up with your own twist or use one of the many commercial blends available online or at your local grocery. Always use glass or stainless steel (not plastic) for brining and non-processed salt, ideally kosher.

For the Buffalo sauce:

2 sticks (½ pound) unsalted butter

1 cup Texas Pete hot sauce

1½ teaspoons ground cayenne pepper

1½ teaspoons mesquite liquid smoke

Juice of 1 fresh lemon

For the blue cheese dressing:

1 cup coarsely crumbled blue cheese

1 cup mayonnaise

1 cup heavy cream

2 tablespoons white wine vinegar

2 tablespoons ground black pepper

2 teaspoons finely minced garlic

2 teaspoons sriracha (or substitute another hot sauce)

¼ teaspoon cayenne pepper

Brine chicken in your favorite poultry brine for 1½ hours. While chicken is brining, prepare the Buffalo sauce and the blue cheese sauce. For the Buffalo sauce, melt the butter over medium heat. Whisk the remaining sauce ingredients together in a medium bowl. When melted, whisk in the butter to combine. For the blue cheese sauce, gently combine all of the ingredients together in a medium bowl, being careful not to overmix. The goal is to have nice chunks of blue cheese in the dressing.

Drain chicken and set aside. Heat canola oil in a deep fryer or deep skillet to 350°F (or over medium high heat if you're using the stove). In a medium bowl, whisk together the buttermilk and the Dijon mustard. Separately, combine the flour, garlic powder, onion powder, salt and pepper in another medium bowl.

Dip the first chicken breast in the buttermilk mixture then place in flour mixture. Coat chicken well with the flour and press firmly. Flip chicken and coat again. Repeat the same process with the remaining chicken breasts.

Gently place the chicken in the deep fryer or skillet (well-spaced, in a single layer). Cook for 4½ minutes and until golden brown. While the chicken is cooking, butter buns and toast on a flat top griddle or medium hot pan. Spread blue cheese dressing on top bun. Place slice of tomato and Bibb lettuce on top bun.

Using tongs, remove the chicken from the hot oil and place on paper-lined plate. Place thermometer in thickest part of chicken to ensure temperature is 165°F. Dunk chicken in Buffalo sauce and let drain well. Place sauced chicken on bottom bun and put sandwich together. Serve hot.

Butcher & Bee

1085 Morrison Drive, upper peninsula
(843) 619-0202
butcherandbee.com
Owner: Michael Shemtov
Executive Chef: Chelsey Conrad

B & B (as it's sometimes called, or simply, "The Bee") executive chef Chelsey Conrad was looking for part-time work in addition to her job at Charleston Grill when she heard about Butcher & Bees's opening five years ago. "They're opening a new local and sustainable craft sandwich shop," said a food and beverage pal. "You'll love it!"

The chef, who draws her inspiration from freshly sourced produce and Middle Eastern (particularly Israeli) flavors, flocked to The Bee. Almost immediately she "fell in love" with the buzz, and was promoted to the lead chef role within a relatively short period of time.

The large, rustic structure on Morrison Drive resembles a barn or shed, which is thoroughly in keeping with its farm-to-table, daily revolving (with some staples) menu.

Sandwiches are at the core, and at the foundation of any great sandwich is the bread. B & B takes that seriously, too, with its in-house bread shop, what Conrad calls the "heart & soul" of the restaurant.

What goes between the buns depends on what's fresh from the farmers that day, (and is by no means exclusively vegetarian), but Conrad loves to put a Middle Eastern spin whenever appropriate. "I feel like food from that region goes hand-in-hand with Southern food and produce. A lot of what we grow here is used in that part of the world. I'm really enjoying making that my piece, my bubble to add to the restaurant."

Her signature and very popular veggie burger, assembled with a green tahini, grilled onions, feta cheese, roasted tomato, and zucchini pickles on brioche, is an excellent example of Conrad's penchant for Middle East-inspired ingredients and flavors, plus vegetarian cooking. It combines beets, mushrooms, green bulgur wheat, and thrashed freekeh (also called farik,) an Israeli grain. Delectable and in high demand, Conrad's veggie burger stays on the menu year-round.

For *The New Charleston Chef's Table,* Conrad shared her luscious Brassica sandwich served on the restaurant's remarkable house-made ciabatta. *Brassica* is a term for the genus of plants in the mustard family which are informally known as cruciferous vegetables. Broccoli and cauliflower, both featured prominently in this sandwich, are part of that family. (Please note, the recipes for the pickled cauliflower, whipped goat cheese and romesco sauce yield more than is needed for just four sandwiches, so you'll have some left over for nibbling and dipping).

BRASSICA SANDWICH

(MAKES 4 SANDWICHES)

1 pound broccoli florets

3 tablespoons kosher or sea salt

Water to cover generously

For the pickled cauliflower:

(MAKES 2 QUARTS)

1 medium head of cauliflower (about 2 pounds) cut into small florets

2 cups apple cider vinegar

1 cup water

¼ cup granulated sugar

2 tablespoons yellow mustard seeds

1 tablespoon dry mustard

1 tablespoon turmeric powder

For the whipped goat cheese:

(MAKES 1 CUP)

The zest of 1 lemon

1 tablespoon chopped fresh thyme

1 tablespoon chopped fresh rosemary

1 teaspoon ground black pepper

1 tablespoon kosher or sea salt

8 ounces chevre or other young goat cheese, at room temperature

For the romesco sauce:

(MAKES ABOUT 2 CUPS)

1 slice country bread (about 1 ounce)

1 12-ounce can roasted red peppers

½ cup toasted, chopped pecans

2 garlic cloves, very finely chopped

1½ tablespoons sherry vinegar

½ teaspoon smoked paprika

½ teaspoon crushed red pepper flakes

1 teaspoon kosher salt

¼ cup extra virgin olive oil

To assemble the sandwiches:

4 ciabatta rolls

Plus 2 tablespoons olive oil and salt and pepper to taste for the final broccoli sauté before compiling the sandwiches

Bring a large pot of water to boil and season heavily with salt. Meanwhile, fill a large mixing bowl with ice water. Working in batches, drop broccoli florets in boiling water and cook for 1 minute. Use a slotted spoon to remove the florets from the pot and into the ice water bowl. Repeat the blanching process with all of the florets. When the florets have cooled drain them well and transfer to a container. Reserve. (These can be prepared a day or two ahead, stored in a sealed container and refrigerated).

Prepare the pickled cauliflower. Divide florets into 2 one-quart jars or 1 larger jar. Combine the rest of the ingredients in a medium saucepan and bring to a boil, stirring occasionally to ensure the sugar dissolves. Cool completely, then pour over cauliflower florets, seal and refrigerate. Allow florets to pickle at least 12 hours, refrigerated, before use.

TIME SAVING
Banana Bread
2.00
Tomato Pie Quiche
2.75
Mini Peach Pie
3.00
Chocolate Croissant
3.50
Phatty Cake
2.00
Blueberry Doughnut
Cherry Lime Pistachio
Pocket Danish 3.50

Prepare the whipped goat cheese. In a medium mixing bowl, stir together all ingredients until well combined. Transfer to container and refrigerate until use. (This can also be made a day or two ahead).

Prepare the romesco sauce. Toast the slice of bread in a toaster oven or a conventional oven until a deep golden brown. Using a food processor, combine the toasted bread and all of the remaining ingredients until ground but still somewhat chunky. Transfer to a container and refrigerate until use. (This can also be made a day or two ahead).

To assemble the sandwiches, slice each ciabatta roll in half horizontally and lightly toast the interior of each side. Spread the top half of each roll with 2 tablespoons of whipped goat cheese and the bottom half of each roll with 1 tablespoon romesco sauce. Set aside the rolls while you prepare the broccoli.

In a large sauté pan, heat 2 tablespoons olive oil over medium high heat for 3 minutes. When hot, add half the broccoli florets and allow the florets to take on some color, about 2 minutes. Toss the florets in the pan and season to taste with salt and ground black pepper. Transfer sautéed broccoli to a plate, then repeat the process with the remaining florets.

Divide the sautéed broccoli between the bottom half of each ciabatta roll. Top the broccoli with a few pieces of pickled cauliflower on each sandwich. Top each sandwich with the other half of the bun and cut each sandwich in half using a serrated knife. Serve immediately.

Minero

153B East Bay Street
(843) 789-2241
minerorestaurant.com
Chef de Cuisine: Wes Grubbs

It seems fitting that Wes Grubbs's first day at Minero, a Mexican restaurant that painstakingly makes its masa in-house and pumps out up to 1,600 hand-pressed tortillas a day, was Cinco de Mayo, the celebration of the Mexican Army's victory at the Battle of Puebla in 1862. The restaurant's name recalls the history of the "taco," the Mexican term miners gave to paper-wrapped gunpowder they used to blast open silver mines, which would eventually become the name of the similarly "wrapped" food.

Like Husk's Travis Grimes, Grubbs was mentored by Sean Brock, first working with him as a butcher at Husk, learning "Southern ways." He didn't anticipate a future in Mexican cooking, until Brock came to him with his fascination of tortillas, tacos, and a love of corn and said, "Here's what I'm thinking, what do you think?" explains Grubbs.

In order to conceive Brock's concept for the restaurant and corresponding menu, Grubbs immersed himself in three solid months of study, pouring over and translating Mexican

cookbooks, and tinkering with recipes using an induction burner. His brain burned with curiosity and ideas to "take what we have and make it our own."

The small, intimate restaurant, rife with whitewashed antique bricks, tin ceilings and exposed rafters, abuts McCrady's and is aromatic with the fragrance of Mexican kitchens with a Southern twist, like the restaurant's silky, nutty benne salsa. The principal ingredient, benne seeds, is a type of sesame seed that was transported to Charleston via African slaves and grown and used heavily in colonial and antebellum kitchens. "It has a Spanish and Lebanese tahini feel to it and also incorporates sorghum's sweetness and (chefs) love of Southern products," says Grubbs.

Excellent for dipping the restaurant's masa tortillas in, it is also a principle component of Minero's mula quesadilla, which is prepared with corn tortillas, cheese, toasted veggies, and a drizzle of the benne salsa. Because the salsa is prepared with a lot of vinegar, it holds easily, chilled, for two to three weeks, according to Grubbs. Morita chilies are smoked red jalapenos and similar to chipotle. Chile de arbol are small, Mexican chili peppers with a very high heat index. If unable to find, substitute with a cayenne pepper or pequin pepper.

MULA QUESADILLA WITH TOASTED VEGETABLES AND BENNE SALSA

(MAKES 6 QUESADILLAS)

For the benne salsa:

(MAKES 1 PINT)

1 morita chile

3 chili de arbol

½ cup vegetable oil

½ cup benne seed

6 cloves garlic, peeled

½ cup medium dice yellow onion

1 tablespoon Mexican oregano

2 allspice berries, toasted and ground (about 1 teaspoon ground allspice)

½ teaspoon cumin, toasted and ground

2 teaspoons kosher or sea salt

4 teaspoons apple cider vinegar

4 tablespoons sorghum

½ cup water

For the quesadilla:

1 medium sweet potato, medium dice

3 pounds (about 12 cups) crimini mushrooms, stemmed and quartered

2 teaspoons vegetable oil

Kosher or sea salt and freshly ground black pepper to taste

1 small white onion, finely diced, rinsed, and patted dry

1 bunch of cilantro, roughly chopped (about 1 cup)

½ cup prepared Benne salsa

1 lime, halved

12 corn tortillas

2 pounds Chihuahua cheese or substitute Muenster

Prepare the salsa first. In a medium sauté pan, add the chilies and the vegetable oil and heat over medium heat until all of the chilies are puffy and darkly toasted (not burnt). Remove the chilies and set aside. Reserve all of the chili oil. In a small saucepan, cover the benne seeds with just enough chili oil to barely cover the top. Fry over medium high heat until golden brown (Don't go too dark, as they will continue to cook off of the heat!) In a small saucepan, heat the remaining chili oil over high heat with the garlic and onion. Cook, stirring occasionally, until the edges are darkened. Add the spices when the onions come off the heat but are still hot. Mix all ingredients, except the water, in a large container, using any remaining chile oil. Blend until smooth, adding water as needed to ease the blending. Salsa should be smooth and pourable but not watery or pasty. Taste and adjust salt, vinegar, and sorghum if necessary.

Preheat oven to 450°F. Arrange the sweet potato and mushrooms on a sheet pan (you may need 2 or 3) in a single layer. Roast in hot oven until the vegetables have wilted and started to crisp on the edges, about 15 minutes. Allow to cool.

Just before assembling quesadillas, heat the oil over medium heat in a sauté pan and add the roasted potatoes and mushrooms. Lightly season with salt and pepper. Heat through for 5 minutes. Separately, place tortillas flat on a lightly greased griddle or large frying pan over medium-high heat until toasted on both sides. Remove from the heat.

To assemble, divide the cheese in a thin layer evenly between all 12 tortillas. Once the cheese has begun to melt, evenly disperse desired amount of onion, cilantro, benne salsa, and sweet potato/mushroom mixture. Finish with a squeeze of lime. Place the remaining cheese tortillas on top and lightly press. Enjoy with mezcal!

HUSK

72 Queen Street, downtown
(843) 577-2500
huskrestaurant.com
Chef/Partner: Sean Brock
Executive Chef: Travis Grimes

Now resident to four Southern cities (Charleston, Nashville, Greenville, and Savannah), Husk's original birthplace was in Charleston at the exceptionally talented hands of James Beard award-winning chef Sean Brock. This restaurant's mission, as its simple, rustic, farm-to-table name implies, is a celebration of local farmers' produce, seafood, meat, poultry, and eggs.

Executive chef Travis Grimes, who's worked side-by-side in kitchens with Brock for many years and at the Husk helm as executive chef since 2015, is a Charleston native with a passion for the Lowcountry and her unique blend of food traditions and products, particularly of the heirloom variety. "Our stamp, everything, is driven by our local farmers. They're bringing in the eggs, raising the chickens, harvesting the seasonal produce," he explains. These items are the building block of the menu which changes daily except for high demand mainstays such as the fried chicken skins, and lettuce-wrapped fried pigs ears, and the exceptional double cheese burger.

Grimes first "experience" with the burger dates back to a party he and Brock were putting together for employees when they were both working the lines at McCrady's (page 162). "Sean wanted a double burger and we decided to grind bacon directly into the meat," Grimes recalls. That bacon and the beef are the building blocks of the burger's unctuous, American cheese gooeyness, and house-made pickles seal the deal with a pert finish to every bite.

Eating one of these is a napkin reaching affair, but don't let the Southern elegance of the restaurant intimidate you. Housed in a late nineteenth-century Charleston family home, it still bears the spirit and mood of a "real home," with floor to ceiling windows and drapes, natural light spinning onto honey-toned antique floors. Next door, there is a diminutive, two-story version former outlay of the main home that's been transformed into the most adorable, craft cocktail and artisanal snack serving bar in town. Settle into one of the deep red banquettes and enjoy yourself. The famous double cheeseburger is on the menu at the bar, too.

Unfortunately, because the recipe and most Husk recipes have been previously published in Sean Brock's award winning *Heritage* (Artisan, 2014) cookbook, I am unable to include it. However, try and piece together your own version based upon Grimes's tips, or better yet, be sure to order this burger beauty when you visit Husk.

Pasta and Rice

We're knee-deep in noodles and deep-seated Latin passion for food and cooking in this chapter, twirling and swirling with the delights of pappardelle, tagliatelle, risotto (a kind of Italian rice), and more. The chefs and restaurants featured here share more than pasta in common. This is an impassioned bunch! Some of these chefs (such as Trattoria Lucca's Ken Vedrinski and Bacco's Michael Scognamiglio) grew up cooking with their Italian grandmothers or grandfathers. All speak of the importance of simplicity, freshness, technique, and love in cooking.

This chapter features several new restaurants, chefs, and recipes since the original release in 2009—a significant reflection of the exciting growth, maturation and heightened diversity and deliciousness happening in The Holy City. Dig into Blake McCormick's bubbly, crusty, homey mac 'n' cheese laced with fish sauce and sherry vinegar; learn expert pasta glazing techniques with 492's Josh Keeler; and discover Indaco's riffs on the elusive perfect carbonara (according to Chef Elliot). The Grocery's Kevin Johnson reinterprets paella and other celebrated rice dishes of the Mediterranean with his Lowcountry seafood and Carolina Gold Rice pilau topped with fresh, fried fish.

Remember, when cooking pasta, the water needs to be well salted, as salty as sea water, in fact. Count on about 3–4 tablespoons per half gallon.

Trattoria Lucca

41-A Bogard at the Corner of Ashe, downtown
(843) 973-3323
luccacharleston.com
Chef/Owner: Ken Vedrinski

This highly decorated celebrity chef (he's garnered three AAA Four Diamond Awards and kudos from *Esquire* and *The New York Times* at previous posts) describes the food at his neighborhood trattoria in the largely residential, rarely-traveled-by-tourists Elliotborough area, as "real."

It is very real, replete with the intimacy, mood, and flavors of the small walled town of Lucca nestled in the rolling hills of Tuscany. "It is just like what you would find in Lucca. There is a restaurant like this just outside the walled part of the city where locals go and the tourists do not," Vedrinski says.

It's the same sapid story here, where college kids, foodie types, and professionals of every class, race, and creed converge to sup on Vedrinski's authentic Tuscan offerings, from antipasti to strozzapreti, in the cozy-yet-sophisticated confines of the hugely inviting space.

Lucca's Sheep's Milk Ricotta Gnudi ("naked pasta") combines Italian duck sausage and Vedrinski's Grandma Volpe's beef spare rib–infused tomato ragu to create ambrosia in a bowl. Scamorza cheese is a fresh or smoked cheese that is similar to mozzarella. If you can't find the former, substitute the latter. If this recipe looks daunting, keep in mind that you can save a lot of time and trouble by using prepared duck sausage and store-bought ricotta or good-quality commercial gnocchi with similar results. It just won't be exactly Grandma Volpe's way!

SHEEP'S MILK RICOTTA GNUDI, HOUSE-MADE ITALIAN DUCK SAUSAGE, GRANDMA VOLPE'S TOMATO RAGU, AND SCAMORZA CHEESE

(SERVES 6)

For the ragu:

2 tablespoons olive oil

2 pounds beef spare ribs

Salt and freshly ground black pepper

1 sweet onion, finely chopped

1 clove garlic, sliced

Pinch of red pepper flakes

2 bay leaves

2 28-ounce cans whole tomatoes, drained and crushed by squeezing between your palm and fingers

½ cup coarsely chopped Parmesan cheese rinds (see Bacco's Parmesan broth, page 109)

For the duck sausage:

1 pound duck legs

1 tablespoon Italian seasoning (a spice blend containing tarragon, sage, basil, marjoram, savory, rosemary, and thyme)

1 tablespoon olive oil

For the ricotta gnudi:

½ gallon whole milk

¼ cup white vinegar

¼ cup sifted pastry flour or all-purpose flour

1 egg, beaten

1 cup grated aged Pecorino cheese

To finish:

1 tablespoon butter

Salt and freshly ground black pepper

½ cup cubed fresh Scamorza cheese or fresh mozzarella

2 tablespoons chopped fresh basil, for garnish (optional)

Pecorino cheese, grated, for garnish (optional)

To prepare the ragu, heat the oil over medium-high heat in a large pot or Dutch oven. Season the ribs lightly on both sides with salt and pepper. When the oil is sizzling, add the ribs to the pot in a single layer. Brown until golden brown (about 5 minutes) and turn, repeating on the second side. Remove the ribs from the pot and set aside. Drain off all but about 3 tablespoons of fat and turn the heat down to medium. Add the onions and garlic, stirring to coat and to pick up brown bits from the bottom of the pan. Season with salt, pepper, and red pepper flakes and add the bay leaves. Cook until onions are just translucent, about 5 minutes. Add the crushed tomatoes to the pot, bring to a boil, and then reduce to a simmer. Return the ribs to the pot and add the Parmesan rinds. Cook very slowly over low heat for 4–6 hours. Remove the ribs, however, as soon as they become very tender but before they are falling apart, after about 3 or 4 hours. (Also remove and discard the bay leaves at this time.) Keep the ribs warm, covered tightly with aluminum foil, in a low oven. Season the sauce to taste and keep warm over low heat.

Next, prepare the duck sausage. Cut the meat away from the bones using a boning knife or paring knife. Discard any sinew or fat. (You can ask your butcher to do the same thing, or buy similarly seasoned prepared duck sausage to save time.) Chop the meat coarsely or grind in a meat grinder set to the smallest size (or ask your butcher to do this). Season the meat with the Italian seasoning. Heat the oil over medium-high heat in a large pot or Dutch oven. Add the seasoned ground duck. Brown gently, stirring occasionally, until evenly browned and cooked

through, 8–10 minutes. Add the reserved ragu to the pot, stirring well to pick up any brown bits. Bring the ragu to a boil and then reduce to a simmer. Keep warm over low heat.

Meanwhile, prepare the gnudi. To make fresh ricotta (you can substitute approximately ½ cup store-bought ricotta if you prefer), bring the milk up to 200°F in a medium-sized pot over medium-high heat. Add the vinegar and stir. The milk will congeal and form a loose kind of ricotta. Strain the mixture through cheesecloth, pressing out and discarding excess fluid. Refrigerate for 1 hour to set the ricotta.

To make the gnudi, combine the ricotta, flour, egg, and grated Pecorino in a mixer fitted with a pastry paddle on low speed, until the dough has just come together, about 5 minutes. Divide the dough into four small balls, space them on a baking sheet, and let rest in the refrigerator for 30 minutes. To form the gnudi, roll each ball into a log with the palm of your hand on a lightly floured surface. The logs should be about 1 or 2 inches in diameter. Cut each log into 1-inch lengths with a pastry cutter. Set aside on a lightly floured surface. To cook, bring a large pot of well-salted water to a boil. Gently add the gnudi and cook for 3–4 minutes, until they float to the surface. Drain well in a colander.

Return the gnudi to the pot and toss with the butter. Season to taste with salt and pepper. Toss lightly with the warm ragu and cubed Scamorza cheese. Serve on individual plates or on a platter, garnishing with fresh basil and a sprinkle of freshly grated Pecorino cheese if desired. Serve 2 or 3 of the warm ribs off to the side of each plate.

Bacco

976 Houston Northcutt Boulevard, Mount Pleasant
(843) 884-6969
baccocharleston.com
Executive Chef/Owner: Michael Scognamiglio

Bad chemistry with a college chemistry class, immediate Italian lineage, a lifetime of good eating, and a passion for Italian cooking eventually aligned the stars to jump-start this young chef's star-worthy culinary career and lead to the opening of this, his first restaurant, at the young age of 25 in 2007. Named after the Roman god of food and wine, Bacco is equal parts convivial and delicious.

Set in a small, relatively spartan space off a well-traveled thoroughfare in Mount Pleasant, Bacco attracts loyal locals from all over greater Charleston for its shining Neapolitan and Venetian fare and the infectious joy Michael takes in pleasing and interacting with his clients. "When I look out in the dining room at night, I always see people conversing back and forth from different tables and they don't even know each other. I like that," he says.

Michael personally selects the wine varietals from Sardinia, Campagna, and Piedmont to pair with his "small but round" menu of select dishes, many of which are loose interpretations of those his father prepared while he was growing up, modified to reflect "restaurant style."

This recipe has Venetian undertones and has been on the restaurant's menu since day one. Don't be put off by risotto. The only techniques required to withdraw the starch from Arborio rice are an initial toast, lots of patient stirring, and warm stock. The rest is a snap. "True Venetian-style *risi e bisi* (rice and peas) should be very runny and almost have a soupy consistency," advises Michael. His version is topped with crispy pancetta.

The tasty Parmesan broth provides an excellent opportunity to use up the rinds of past Parmesan cheese rounds you've hopefully been storing in your freezer. (If not, ask the cheese cutter at your grocery for a bunch, or substitute chicken or vegetable broth for a milder, less cheesy flavor.)

RISI E BISI (RICE AND PEAS)

(SERVES 6)

For the Parmesan broth:

½ gallon water

½ pound Parmesan rinds

1 bay leaf

1½ teaspoons whole black peppercorns

¼ onion

For the risotto:

1 cup diced pancetta (salt-cured Italian bacon, available in most grocery stores)

2 tablespoons olive oil

3 cups Arborio rice (a round, Italian rice with a high starch content)

1 cup fresh or frozen peas

2 tablespoons butter

½ cup freshly grated Parmesan

Salt and freshly ground black pepper to taste

To prepare the broth, combine all of the broth ingredients in a large pot and simmer for 30–45 minutes over medium heat, stirring on occasion, to prevent the cheese rinds from sticking to the bottom of the pot. Remove from the heat and strain broth through a fine-mesh strainer. Reserve warm or cool and refrigerate or freeze until you're ready to prepare the risotto. (The broth should keep, refrigerated in an airtight container, for up to a week and in the freezer for several months.)

To prepare the risotto, heat a medium sauté pan over medium-high heat and add the pancetta. Cook, tossing occasionally, until the pancetta is golden brown and crispy, about 5 minutes. Remove from the pan and drain on paper towels. Meanwhile, heat the olive oil in a medium pot over medium-high heat. Add the rice and sauté (toasting the rice) for 30 seconds, stirring constantly. (This "wakes up" the rice and prepares it for the all-important broth absorption process.) Add about 2½ cups of the warm Parmesan broth, or enough to just cover the rice, and cook over medium heat for 15 minutes, stirring constantly. Add additional broth in ¼-cup increments, if needed to keep the rice moist. Add the peas and continue cooking for another 2–3 minutes, stirring constantly and adding small amounts of broth if the rice appears to be getting dry.

The risotto will need 20–25 minutes to cook to al dente. When done, remove from the heat and stir in the butter and grated Parmesan. Season to taste with salt and pepper. Serve in shallow bowls and sprinkle each bowl with pancetta. Serve immediately. Risotto waits for no one!

INDACO

526 King Street, downtown
(843) 872-6828
indacocharleston.com
Executive Chef: Elliot Cusher

Indaco (the Italian word for indigo, one of the wealth building blocks of colonial Charleston's economy) is another excellent hot wood-fired pizza destination around town. Indaco adds a delectable dash of hand-crafted pasta, housemade salumi and cured sausages, all served in a sophisticated, sexy, and romantic space on Upper King Street.

Executive chef Elliot Cusher (pronounced like pusher with a "c"), is a Charleston native and Johnson & Wales grad who has spent time in several kitchens in the area, as well as a few stints in Miami and New Orleans, before leaving and coming back home to Charleston. He blends his talent and experience at Indaco with what he describes as "traditional and contemporary distinctly Italian cuisine using local and regional products as daily inspiration."

"Seventy percent of the menu is traditional, such as our Bolognese (but we add prosciutto and chicken liver) and the other thirty percent is contemporary, such as our veal sweet breads, which is really a very liberal interpretation of veal Marsala. I really like to have fun and flex our kitchen muscles a little bit. But, the older I get, the more I realize that simple is elegant and less is more. That's what we strive to do here and do well," says Cusher.

He draws from his year spent backpacking about Europe and working in kitchens there, including a pass through Italy, as well as constant inspiration from local fishmonger, poultry, meat, and produce sources. "We're so blessed to have that here in Charleston. We've got a fishmonger that will call and tell us what's in, and it's always so beautiful, and that's what we're putting on the menu that night."

The Black Pepper Tagliatelli is a staple from the restaurant's opening days. It is one of four items that remains virtually unchanged on the menu and is always offered because, as Cusher rightly says, it is simple and classic. It is also fabulously delicious and easily prepared in home kitchens. He loves the recipe for the home cook because it "is a good start for understanding how to properly glaze pasta." He intentionally wrote the recipe in "kitchen vernacular in a playful manner," so that's how I've left it for you. Enjoy!

Here's a few of his tips on ingredients and modifications:

"At the restaurant we use tessa instead of pancetta, a cured pork belly product that is made with an insane amount of garlic, black peppercorns, and red wine. Pancetta is a very similar product, but more readily found. We make our own tessa and it takes about two weeks from start to finish. We also make our pasta fresh with loads of ground black pepper. De Cecco is a great brand to substitute. De Cecco has dried pasta with eggs that is awesome, but is not the same thing as regular dried pasta. Normal dried pasta is made with semolina and water. Make sure to get the stuff with the eggs in it. Usually takes less time to cook as well as being softer on the palate due to a finer grind of wheat flour."

BLACK PEPPER TAGLIATELLE WITH CURED EGG YOLK, PANCETTA AND PARMESAN CHEESE

(SERVES 6)

1 cured egg yolk (see method directions)

2 cups pancetta cubed into ¼-inch dice, rendered (see method directions)

2 pounds dried De Cecco Tagliatelle (or another egg pasta brand)

3 tablespoons to ¼ cup kosher or sea salt for cooking the pasta

3 tablespoons whole unsalted butter

1 cup brown chicken stock

¼ cup reserved pasta cooking water

½ cup freshly grated Parmesan cheese

¼ cup thinly sliced chives

1½ teaspoons coarsely ground black peppercorns

Sea or kosher salt to taste

Fresh lemon juice to taste

1 raw egg yolk (optional)

For the cured egg yolk, take approximately 2 cups of salt and pour it onto a small dish to cover completely. Before you crack the egg, use large end to make a small indention in the salt. Then crack egg and separate yolk and white. Place the yolk in the salt indention and cover completely with some of the excess salt on the plate. Wrap plate container in plastic wrap and refrigerate for two days. After two days gently remove yolk and wash with cool running water. Place on elevated resting rack and dry at room temperature for several days (3–5 days) until the egg is firm enough to be grated. Once fully dried, store the egg at room temperature. If refrigerated, the yolk will become gummy and mealy. Ain't nobody got time for that!

Cut and render the pancetta. We cut ours into the pieces about as big as half my pinky. How you cut yours is up to you. By the time it renders out, it is about half the size from when we started. I like to dice it all and put it into a pan in an oven around 350°F. We check on it about every 10 minutes and stir, making sure there is plenty of surface area for the heat to make contact. If your pan is loud and angry, turn down the heat. You want to cook it gently. Also don't cook it until it is like a piece of crispy bacon. You still want some fat to render out in the sauté pan as you're picking up the pasta.

Next, bring a large pot of heavily salted ("salty like the sea") water to a fast simmer. I don't like hard boils with this type of pasta. It's delicate and will rip it to pieces. Drop the pasta in, making sure there is plenty of room in the pot for the pasta to move around.

In a separate, large sauté pan, brown the butter with the rendered pancetta, over medium high heat. Once butter has browned, whisk in the chicken stock and remove from heat. The butter will emulsify with the chicken stock.

Check the pasta and cook to desired doneness. Some people like more al dente than others. Just make sure it's not raw in the middle. Only way you are going to do that is by tasting it. Taste, taste, taste! I can't stress it enough. Pull pasta out of the water and shake to slightly dry. Reserve ¼ cup of the pasta cooking water for finishing the sauce. Starch from the pasta water helps tighten your sauce, as well as a dusting of parmesan cheese.

Now it's time to add the drained pasta to the butter, chicken stock, and pancetta sauce in the sauté pan. Vigorously toss the pasta and add the reserved pasta water and the cheese. The emulsified sauce should beautifully glaze the pasta and the cheese will give it added body and flavor. You know your sauce work is correct when you stick a spoon in it and can run your finger down the back of the spoon and the sauce holds beautifully. If you don't feel comfortable tossing your hard work and risking it ending up all over your kitchen floor then I recommend gently stirring with a wooden spoon. Just don't beat the hell out of it.

At the very end we like to adjust seasoning with lemon juice and maybe some more Parmesan. We use Parmesan like salt sometimes, but too much will ruin your beautiful glaze on your pasta. Trust me when I say there is such a thing as too much cheese. We also add in the chives and this is the time to add the black pepper to taste. Taste it, don't just blindly go adding it. Have you had the same black peppercorns in your pantry for the last four years? It is not going to taste the same as beautifully toasted fresh peppercorns. This is where your personal taste comes into play. Start with a smaller amount. You can always add more.

To finish, plate the pasta in a large serving bowl with more chives on top, more freshly grated Parmesan, grated cured egg, and the raw egg yolk for added body in the pasta once it is thoroughly mixed in. Serve warm.

492

492 King Street, downtown
(843) 203-6338
492king.com
Executive Chef: Josh Keeler

Abandoned since monster Hurricane Hugo in 1989, this former nineteenth century clothing store recently received a massive, beautifully crafted facelift and a new name reflecting its location on restaurant popular Upper King Street. Reflections of the building's heritage take the form of a button wall of sous-vide leeks photographs and a fabric ceiling of a circa 1902 Charleston city map in the downstairs dining room.

Weaving wonders at the culinary loom at 492 is executive chef Josh Keeler, a native of Scranton, Pennsylvania. The super talented chef is enamored with simplicity, sourcing, and rice, specifically Charleston gold rice, an heirloom grain with colonial and antebellum era roots. "I knew very little about it before moving here. I'd never really had great rice before and I never realized how truly satisfying it can be when perfectly cooked with very little butter and very little salt," says Keeler.

His constantly evolving mission as a chef really goes to the heart of sourcing and minimalism on the plate. "I buy the best possible ingredients and try to mess with it as little as possible and showcase it for what it is. Think, how do you make a carrot taste more like a carrot, the best carrot you've ever had?"

A prime pasta example is Keeler's interpretation of carbonara, which he describes as "cheese, eggs and something salty." He and his wife had a version at Prune in NYC and he thought it would be something great to eat in the morning. At 492, it is showcased on the Sunday brunch menu and Keeler uses braised short ribs (as in the following recipe), lamb, lamb shoulder, rib ends, whatever's left-over and makes sense. "It's kind of great for the home cook who may have some left-over pot roast and is trying to figure out how to turn it into a second meal."

The short ribs recipe makes more than you will need for the carbonara. Chef Keeler recommends either saving some to serve with eggs in the morning or an impromptu taco night for the family. For the grated Parmesan in the actual carbonara, he recommends buying a whole piece and grating it at home for better quality control.

CARBONARA WITH BUCATINI, PARMESAN, SHORT RIB, EGG

(SERVES 6 + SHORT RIB LEFT-OVERS)

For the braised short ribs:

3 pounds boneless chuck short ribs (found at any butcher shop or grocery story)

2 teaspoons kosher or sea salt

1 tablespoon freshly ground black pepper

2 ounces grapeseed oil (or substitute vegetable oil or peanut oil)

2 carrots peeled, coarsely chopped

2 medium yellow onions, coarsely chopped

1 head/bunch (about 12 stalks) celery, washed thoroughly and coarsely chopped

1 head garlic, root end removed

2 tablespoons tomato paste

2 cups good quality dry white wine (Chef says any variety is ok, just no sweet wines!)

4 cups chicken stock, either homemade or low-sodium store bought

2 bay leaves

1 teaspoon freshly ground black pepper

Start with a Dutch oven or other oven safe dish, preferably with a lid, but definitely one that can be placed on the stove top. Preheat oven to 300°F and place the Dutch oven on the stove top over medium heat. While pan is heating, season the short ribs with a generous amount of salt and freshly cracked black pepper. Add the oil to the pan once it is hot and place the short ribs inside. Brown the short ribs evenly on all sides until caramelized (about 4 minutes each side). As they are caramelized, remove them from the pan and set aside.

Add the carrots, onions, celery, and garlic to the warm pan, stirring to break up any browned bits, cooking over medium heat. The vegetables will release their water into the pan. Cook this liquid off and the vegetables will slowly begin to caramelize, after about 15 minutes. Once the vegetables are lightly colored (but not burned!), add the tomato paste and mix thoroughly. The paste will turn a deep red color. At this point, add the wine to the pan and reduce it until only half of it remains. Add the seared short ribs back to the pan resting on the bed of vegetables and turn the heat off. Poor in the stock and cover the pan, either with the lid or tightly fitting aluminum foil. Place the pan in the oven for about 2 hours, but check progress after 1 hour.

You want the short ribs to be tender and just about to fall apart with a little pressure, but not falling apart on their own. Remove short ribs from oven and let them cool in their own juices. Overnight is best but a few hours will work, as well. After cooling, pull the short ribs apart into bite size pieces and reserve for the carbonara. (Note: Any left-over short ribs can be refrigerated and stored in a sealed container for several days for future use.)

For the carbonara:

1 1-pound package dried bucatini pasta (Rustichella d'Abruzzo brand is Chef Keeler's favorite)

3 tablespoons kosher or sea salt (or as Chef Keeler says, "enough until it tastes like an ocean")

2 whole eggs

2 egg yolks

2 tablespoons extra virgin olive oil

1½–2 cups of prepped, shredded short ribs

Reserved cooked pasta and 1 cup of pasta water

Sea salt or kosher salt and freshly ground black pepper, to taste

½ cup freshly grated Parmesan cheese

Place a large pot of water on the stove and add the salt. Bring water to a rolling boil over high heat. Once boiling, add the dried pasta and cook for 8–12 minutes, until al dente or "soft but with a little bit of chew." Drain in a colander, reserving 1 cup of the pasta water to finish the sauce. Set the pasta aside.

In a small bowl, whisk two whole eggs with two egg yolks until incorporated. Place a large sauté pan on stove top over low heat and add the olive oil. Add the short rib to the pan and lightly sauté until warmed through. Add the cooked bucatini plus the reserved pasta water to the short rib pan and mix until all the pasta and short ribs are incorporated. Season to taste with salt and pepper.

Turn off the heat under the pan. While continually stirring, add the eggs to the pasta. The pasta should be warm but not hot. You want the eggs to coat the pasta and slightly thicken, but not cook or scramble. The eggs should be cooked and slightly thickened within thirty seconds. Once cooked, add the grated cheese. Serve to guests immediately.

The Grocery

4 Cannon Street (near King), downtown
(843) 302-8825
thegrocerycharleston.com
Owner/Executive Chef: Kevin Johnson

After working for almost twenty years in food and beverage, including stints at The Inn at Little Washington in D.C., S.N.O.B. (see page 170), and Anson (see page 135), James Beard Award semifinalist for Best Chef Southeast (2014) Kevin Johnson was able to make his dream of opening his own restaurant a reality. With his wife, Susan, by his side, offering "lots of support, encouragement, administrative and creative support," their Grocery restaurant baby was born in 2011. "It was wonderful to do it all on our own, no outside financing or anything. It has been really rewarding," says Johnson.

Located near King, the massive space has been a beacon for heaping servings of Johnson's signature style, what he describes as diverse and evolving, and ultimately "new American." He balances the signature ingredients of the Lowcountry with a sense of place, increasingly taking cues from Mediterranean cooking and a heightened use of vegetables and seafood.

For example, his interpretation of pilau (rice cooked in a seasoned broth), is prepared with Carolina Gold's nutty, distinctively flavored and textured rice, and infused with the seafood flavors of the Lowcountry. "It is quintessentially Charleston. In the Mediterranean, everyone has a way of showcasing seafood, a bouillabaisse in France and paella in Spain. In Charleston, we have Carolina Gold rice and seafood. They all come together beautifully in this dish," says Johnson.

Like many recipes, this one was born of abundance, a surplus of crabs from a crabber in nearby Bull's Bay. Johnson had to come up with something using the crab that was interesting and approachable. "At first it was crab, fried fish, rice and peas. People loved it and when crab season ended, we started doing it without crab, and added shrimp and clams, instead. Fried local fish on top is the crispy finish."

Carolina Gold rice is an aromatic heirloom grain with a buttery, nutty flavor, a kind of Lowcountry twist on basmati, with a history dating to colonial and antebellum eras in Charleston. It can be found in many local groceries when visiting Charleston and multiple sources online. Field peas are also indigenous to Charleston (and other parts of the world). They can be substituted with green peas or another legume if unavailable in your area.

LOWCOUNTRY SEAFOOD PILAU

(SERVES 6–8)

For the pilau base:

1 teaspoon olive oil

1 teaspoon fennel seeds

Pinch red pepper flakes

½ small head fennel, cored and finely diced

1 small yellow onion, minced

1 small carrot, peeled and diced

2 small ribs celery, diced

4 cloves garlic, minced

Kosher or sea salt and freshly ground black pepper

4–6 threads saffron

8 sprigs fresh thyme, leaves picked and minced

2 tablespoons tomato paste

½ cup dry white wine

4 cups fish stock

1½ cups shrimp stock

For the pilau:

2-2½ pounds mild, thin fish (Chef recommends snapper, triggerfish, sheepshead and flounder as all good options), cut into 4–ounce pieces

Kosher or sea salt and freshly ground black pepper

Buttermilk, as needed to cover

6 cups canola oil

4 cups prepared pilau base, plus 1 cup

2½ cups cooked field peas

1 cup stewed tomatoes

6 cups cooked Carolina Gold rice

24 littleneck clams, scrubbed and rinsed

24 large shrimp, heads removed and deveined, shells-on

For cornmeal seasoning:

2 cups stone ground white cornmeal, as needed

Kosher or sea salt and freshly ground black pepper to taste

1 bunch Italian parsley, leaves (discard stems) minced

8 sprigs tarragon, picked and minced

12 sprigs chives, snipped

3 tablespoons minced chervil

1 lemon, cut into wedges

Prepare the pilau base. In a large pot, over medium heat, toast the fennel seeds and chili flakes in olive oil. After toasted and fragrant, add fennel, onion, carrot, celery, and garlic. Season with a little salt and pepper and sweat until tender, about 5 minutes. Add saffron and thyme. Add tomato paste and cook about 5–10 minutes. Deglaze with white wine and reduce by half. Add the fish and shrimp stocks and let simmer for about an hour. Season with salt and pepper as needed, remove from heat, and use immediately in pilau or chill until ready to use. (The base can be made up to two days ahead and stored sealed, in the refrigerator.)

Prepare the pilau. Season fish with salt and pepper, cover fish with buttermilk and let stand for about 30 minutes. Pour the oil into a large pot and heat to 350°F over medium-high heat (for frying fish). Meanwhile, heat about 4 cups of pilau base in a large pot with the field peas and stewed tomatoes and bring to a simmer. Add rice and gently heat through. Add more base if needed. Keep warm.

Bring the additional 1 cup of pilau base to a boil over high heat in a large sauté pan big enough to hold the clams and shrimp. Add clams and cover with a tight fitting lid. Once clams start opening, add shrimp and cover again. Cook until shrimp

are cooked through, about 3 minutes. Keep warm. Meanwhile, remove fish from buttermilk, dredge in seasoned cornmeal and fry in batches until golden and cooked through, about 3 minutes depending on the thickness of the fish. Drain on wire rack. Gently mix the remaining fresh herbs into the hot rice. Arrange shrimp and clams around the plated rice. Top with crispy fish. Serve hot, lined with lemon wedges for squeezing.

EVO PIZZA

1075 E. Montagu Avenue, North Charleston (at Park Circle)
(843) 225-1796
evopizza.com
Chef: Blake McCormick

When EVO (which stands for "extra virgin oven") co-founders Matt McIntosh and Ricky Hacker started carting their mobile wood-fired pizza oven through local farmers' markets and popular gathering spaces in 2003, their legions of fans for the crispy, bubbly crusted Neapolitan-style pizza topped with seasonal local produce grew like wildfire. Born as a dream when the men worked together at FIG (see page 38), it would be just two years before they set up shop at a cosmopolitan chic brick and mortar space in the trendy Park Circle neighborhood in North Charleston.

Soon the talk of the town, word was spreading not just to customers, but to the food and beverage crowd. While working as a waitress at High Cotton, then Charleston Art Institute culinary student Blake McCormick was interested in kitchen work. The High Cotton sous chef told her, "You've got to go talk to Matt and Ricky." Even though she was working full-time at High Cotton and going to school, she started at EVO working as *garde manger*, three lunches a week.

Before long, her hard work paid off and she was offered the head chef (she doesn't like the term "executive") position and started putting her brand on the EVO name in 2011. A kind of every woman, the self-termed "reluctant chef" works hard at keeping her well-oiled machine in a constant state of repair and motion. She plans and writes daily specials for lunch and dinner, picks up produce at farms and even has some farmers drop them off directly at her home doorstep. "In the kitchen, I work really hard on keeping thing simple and straightforward and run a really tight ship, trying to address and teach what we're capable of doing well and especially, consistently. You can tell when you eat, see a dish, if it's been put together with love. That's what we strive for," says an exuberant McCormick.

Her very popular wood-fired mac 'n' cheese is a riff on a Michael Ruhlman recipe, but she changes it up quite a bit by adding fish sauce, sherry vinegar, and a variation in the compilation of the béchamel sauce and the cheeses. It's a restaurant staple. She tucks it in the hottest part of the oven at the restaurant to get that crusty layer, but insists it can be done just as well at home. "My mother makes it from this recipe all the time!"

EVO MAC & CHEESE

(SERVES 5–7)

1 pound dried pasta (EVO uses Creste di Gallo brand mohawk macaroni)

For the onion and shallot puree:

1 tablespoon unsalted butter

1 large sweet onion, chopped

2 small shallots, chopped

LOCAL IS BEST
AmbroseFarm WADMALAW, SC
Frothy Beard North Charleston, SC
GEECHIE BOY EDISTO, SC
COAST BREWERY NORTH CHARLESTON, SC
HARVIN MEATS KINGSTREE, SC
Johns Island, SC
HOLY CITY North Charleston, SC
King of POPS North Charleston, SC
Kurios Farm MONCKS Corner, SC
OUR LOCAL SC Purveyors
LEGARE FARM Johns Island, SC
RIVERDOG RIDGELAND, SC
MEPKIN ABBEY MONCKS CORNER, SC
ROSE BANK Johns Island, SC
REBELLION FARM RAVENEL, SC
SPLITCREEK FARMS ANDERSON, SC

Specials
Pimento & Pickles
Duck Confit & Tomato panini
Potatoes & Calabrese Pizza
EXTRA
CHECK OUT EVO CRAFT BAKERY
OPEN 7-4 MONDAY-SATURDAY
Located Behind us
Desserts
King of Pops Popsicles
SPLIT CREEK FARMS

For the béchamel sauce:

3 tablespoons unsalted butter
3 tablespoons all-purpose flour
1½ cups whole milk
1 tablespoon sherry vinegar
1 tablespoon fish sauce
2 teaspoons dry mustard
½ teaspoon cracked black pepper
¼ teaspoon ground cayenne
¼ teaspoon Spanish paprika
Prepared onion and shallot puree

½ pound sharp cheddar, grated
¼ pound Havarti, grated
¼ pound Gouda, grated
¼ pound Parmigiano-Reggiano, grated
2 tablespoons unsalted butter or olive oil for greasing the pan

Preheat oven to 400°F. Cook the pasta for 7 minutes in heavily salted, boiling water, until just al dente. Drain well in a colander, rinse and set aside.

Prepare the onion and shallot puree. In a heavy bottomed pot, melt butter on medium high. Add onions and shallots once butter is melted. Cook, stirring regularly until onions and shallots are caramelized and soft. Season with a generous pinch of salt. Put warm mixture in a blender and puree until smooth. Reserve.

Prepare the béchamel. In a heavy bottomed pot, melt butter on medium. Using a flat wooden spatula, stir and slowly add in flour. Continually stir to cook the roux and avoid scorching, lower heat if necessary. Cook until it develops a nutty toasty aroma. Slowly add in milk and whisk making sure that that flour is not sticking. Cook until thickened. Add the sherry vinegar, fish sauce, dry mustard, black pepper, cayenne, and Spanish paprika. Add in all of the onion and shallot puree. Whisk to combine. Taste and adjust seasonings as needed. Reserve warm.

Put it all together. In a large bowl, combine the cheddar, Havarti and Gouda cheeses. Separately, in another large bowl combine pasta, béchamel sauce and ¾ of the combined grated cheeses. Stir until evenly distributed. Grease a glass 9 x 13 baking dish with butter or oil. Spread pasta mixture evenly, top with remaining cheese and finish with a generous grating of Parmigiano-Reggiano.

Cover with foil and put in oven. Bake until bubbly and hot throughout (30-40 minutes) Uncover and turn oven to a low broil, cook until top is browned. Remove from oven, let rest for 10 minutes before serving.

SEAFOOD

An eternally proud bunch, Charlestonians are fond of referring to the brackish waters that form the port and envelop the peninsula and islands as the place "where the Ashley and Cooper Rivers meet to form the Atlantic." That may be disputable, but what is not is the fact that Charleston is literally surrounded by water—rivers, an ocean, marshes, tributaries—and in those waters resides a rich population of fish and crustaceans unique to the climate and geography of the area. Triggerfish, wreckfish, red drum, and other fish, along with the Lowcountry's famous bounty of briny shrimp and oysters, fall temptingly into the talented hands of the chefs in this chapter, who demand local fresh fish in their kitchens. "Simplicity" was the across-the-board battle cry in talking with these chefs about working with fish, but "boring" was most decidedly not.

Tantalizing new additions include Mike Lata's smart and whimsical fish schnitzel, prepared with triggerfish that is breaded and fried and finished with a zippy sunchoke, butter, lemon, and caper sauce at The Ordinary. Coda del Pesce does a refreshing twist on an Italian classic, in Ken Vedrinski's Picatta of Cherry Point swordfish "Torcino Style." Snapper at Chez Nous takes a gentle olive oil bath and is dotted with an assortment of delicate spring vegetables, while Zero George's treatment of the same fish is layered with a decadent crawfish rich "nage" and the richness of chanterelles and Beech mushrooms. High Thyme's seared scallops swim in a curried carrot puree, laced with colorful roasted beets and creamy goat cheese. Fried, seared, poached or simmered, Charleston chefs punctuate their skills, passion, and ingenuity in utilizing some of the area's most revered jewels from local waters.

Bowen's Island Restaurant

1970 Bowen's Island Road, Folly Island
(843) 795-2757
Bowensisland.biz
Owner: Robert Barber

Equally legendary for its succulent steamed oysters and never-ending graffiti stockpile, Bowen's is a tumbledown, ultra-casual place. It's surrounded by piles of white, half-forgotten oyster shells and drenched with palpable memories of easy times spent at the water's edge drinking beer and slurping down oysters with good friends.

Before it was a restaurant, Bowen's was a fish camp where owner Robert Barber's grandparents cooked fish and shrimp in a skillet and roasted oysters over an open fire for their overnight camp guests. Robert took over the business upon his grandmother's death. By that time, the restaurant had morphed into a Lowcountry must-do-before-you-die legend. Indeed, Robert was honored with a James Beard Award in 2006, which deemed Bowen's an American classic.

The simple menu here features mostly boiled and fried local seafood along with another Lowcountry classic, Frogmore Stew. Also called "Lowcountry Boil" and "Beaufort Stew," it originally got its name from a section of St. Helena Island near Beaufort (about an hour and a half south of Charleston) where the dish was created. For Bowen's version, Robert insists upon Hillshire Farm smoked kielbasa ("It's got more bite and texture," he says) and not overcooking the shrimp. "You can cook all of 'em (corn, potatoes, sausage) too long, but if you overcook the shrimp, it's messed up," he says. He's right. Stir the shrimp in at the very end and let the heat from the broth cook them just right before serving. This is a comforting meal that cooks in a single pot in minutes.

BOWEN'S ISLAND FROGMORE STEW

(SERVES 6)

6–8 cups cold water

3 tablespoons Old Bay Seasoning

Dash of Texas Pete Hot Sauce (or your preferred brand)

1 stick (¼ pound) unsalted butter (optional)

1½ pounds new red potatoes

1½–2 pounds Hillshire Farm smoked kielbasa, cut into 1- to 2-inch lengths

6 ears corn, shucked and broken in half

2 pounds (20-24 count) shell-on fresh shrimp

Place the cold water, Old Bay Seasoning, hot sauce, and butter, if using, in a large pot. (The amount of water depends on the size of your pot. You should have enough space to let the ingredients breathe and move and enough water to barely cover them.)

Bring the seasoned water to a boil over high heat. Once boiling, add the potatoes and cook for 10–15 minutes or until the potatoes are soft when pierced with a fork. Reduce the heat to medium-high. Add the kielbasa and corn and cook for another 5 minutes. Increase the heat to high and bring the mixture back to a boil. (It must be at a boil before adding the shrimp.) Add the shrimp all at once and remove pot from the heat. Stir gently to mix in the shrimp and keep watching until the shrimp start to turn pink. Drain the stew in a large colander and return to the pot. Serve immediately on a large platter or on individual plates; Robert uses a rustic copper or wooden bowl to serve at the restaurant. Across the Lowcountry, this dish is often served on tables covered with newspaper. Try it at home for an especially authentic feeling.

THE CHARLESTON BUMP

The Charleston Bump, where wreckfish thrive, rises off the surrounding Blake Plateau, which is located roughly 100 miles offshore from South Carolina and Georgia. Depths here range from an astonishing 1,300 to 3,000 feet of tumultuous water, swirling with eddies and rapid, mean currents. It makes for an unusual combination of tough fishing and a happy habitat for wreckfish, which embrace its spooky universe of deep-water corals and caves. It's also the exclusive spawning and hunting ground for wreckfish in the U.S., a wholly sustainable fish that is monitored by the state and federal governments. The fish is named for its fondness for lurking in and around wreckage and debris.

Hank's

10 Hayne Street, downtown
(843) 723-3474
hanksseafoodrestaurant.com
Executive Chef: Tim Richardson

Local entrepreneur extraordinaire Hank Holliday wanted to create a really good seafood restaurant in downtown's historic district when he opened his eponymous restaurant, Hank's. Holliday was inspired by his memories of a long-defunct Charleston restaurant classic, Henry's, which was of the white tablecloth seafood variety.

Hank's special blend of Southern and Lowcountry contemporary cuisine is served in a manly setting awash in dark, gleaming woods, leather, and yes, white linen tablecloths. An expansive raw bar and a practically life-size mural of Hank decked out in a white apron, holding a massive lobster, dominate, contributing to the old-world men's club feel of the place.

Long-standing Chef de Cuisine (prior to being promoted to his current position), executive chef Tim Richardson embraces simple preparations of local seafood. This recipe showcases Charleston's very own wreckfish (see The Charleston Bump sidebar, page 127), a meaty, moist fish remotely related to grouper and snapper (which can be substituted when wreckfish is unavailable) in flavor and texture.

Wreckfish with Green Tomato, Sweet Corn, and Blue Cheese Vinaigrette

(SERVES 4)

For the vinaigrette:

1 cup green tomatoes, cored and chopped
1 medium ear sweet corn, shucked
¼ cup chopped scallions
2 tablespoons chopped chives
Salt and freshly ground black pepper to taste
1 cup double-strength chicken stock (prepare by reducing 2 cups of unsalted chicken stock)
¼ cup champagne vinegar or apple cider vinegar
½ cup extra-virgin olive oil
¼ cup crumbled blue cheese

For the fish:

4 6-ounce wreckfish fillets

Salt and freshly ground black pepper to taste

2 tablespoons olive oil

2 tablespoons butter

Preheat the oven to 350°F. To prepare the vinaigrette, core the tomatoes and cut into medium dice. Roast the corn on the cob in the oven for 20 minutes, or until golden brown. Allow to cool. Cut the corn from the cob and place in a medium bowl with the diced tomato. Add the scallions and chives and season with salt and pepper. Cover this mixture with the chicken stock and vinegar. Mix gently, then whisk in the olive oil and blue cheese. Add salt and pepper to taste.

Season the fish on both sides with salt and pepper. Heat a large skillet over medium-high heat and add the olive oil and butter. When sizzling, add the wreckfish fillets in a single, well-spaced layer. Cook for 4–6 minutes (depending on the thickness of the fillets), turn, and repeat. Serve immediately on individual plates, topped with a generous serving of the vinaigrette.

Muse

82 Society Street, downtown
(834) 577-1102
charlestonmuse.com
Chef: Joaquin Bustos

This eclectic Mediterranean gem looks to Pompeii and the Villa of the Mysteries' famous frescoes, along with the myriad cuisines and ingredients of the Mediterranean, as its multifarious muse. Murals of the muses of Spain, Italy, France, and Greece adorn this rambling circa-1850 dollhouse like so many rays of merry light on a sparkling sea. Situated on a quiet, residential street in the heart of downtown, Muse embodies intimacy and whimsy in a colorful, fell swoop.

At Muse, ingredients from various Mediterranean countries are thoughtfully merged. This recipe gets inspiration from Southerners' penchant for fried seafood, but the fish is kept whole (bones removed), the way that Mediterranean sea bass ("bronzini") is commonly served in Europe. It's a compelling presentation and just fabulous with the acidic edge of orange and smoothness of pureed cauliflower. If you can't find bronzini, substitute red snapper, which has a similar mild flavor and creamy texture. Because removing the bones while leaving the head and tail intact is a challenging notion for most home cooks, just leave the bones in and ask your fishmonger to gut the fish for you and, if possible, remove the spine and ribs. Alternatively, you could fry fillets following the directions below.

Lightly Fried Whole Mediterranean Sea Bass over Cauliflower Puree with an Orange Saffron Butter Sauce and Fried Basil

(SERVES 4)

For the cauliflower puree:

1 head cauliflower

¼ cup canola oil

Sea or kosher salt and freshly ground black pepper

For the butter sauce:

2 cups fresh-squeezed orange juice (do not use concentrate)

1 cup white wine

1 shallot, thinly sliced

10 fennel seeds, toasted briefly to release flavor

½ teaspoon saffron

5 whole black peppercorns

1 bay leaf

Salt and freshly ground black pepper to taste

2 sticks (½ pound) cold butter, cut into 16 tablespoon-sized pieces

For the fish and garnish:

8 cups canola oil

16 fresh basil leaves

4 small whole bronzini (Mediterranean sea bass), gutted

Salt and freshly ground black pepper to taste

2 cups semolina

To prepare the cauliflower puree, cut the cauliflower into quarters and remove any tough stems from the center of each quarter's core. Break off the florets using your fingers. Heat canola oil in a large sauté pan over medium heat and add the cauliflower. Season with salt and pepper once the cauliflower hits the pan, and cook until tender, stirring occasionally, 10–12 minutes. Be careful not to brown the cauliflower. When cauliflower is tender, transfer to a food processor and puree until smooth and light. Keep puree warm over a gently simmering water bath.

To prepare the butter sauce, combine the orange juice, white wine, shallot, fennel seed, saffron, peppercorns, and bay leaf in a medium saucepan and bring to a boil over high heat. Reduce the heat to medium-high and continue to cook until the sauce is reduced by two-thirds. Season with salt and pepper. Reduce the heat to medium. To finish, gradually incorporate the cold butter, 2 tablespoons at a time, by whisking the butter into the warm sauce to form an emulsion. The sauce should not ever boil, and it should become cohesive and frothy with a brilliant orange color. Continue adding butter until it is all incorporated. Strain the sauce through a fine-mesh sieve and keep warm over a gently simmering water bath.

To cook the garnish and fish, heat 8 cups of canola oil in a large pot over medium-high heat to 400°F. When the oil has reached that temperature, throw the basil leaves in all at once and fry for 15 seconds. They will sizzle and pop and turn a brilliant green. Remove the leaves with a slotted spoon and drain on paper towels.

Season the fish on both sides. Place the flour in a shallow bowl and dredge the fish in the flour, tapping off any excess. Fry the fish, one at a time, until cooked through and golden brown (2–3 minutes for a 1½-pound bronzini, less for fillets).

To serve, evenly distribute the warm cauliflower puree among four plates. Place the fish on top of the puree. Spoon several tablespoons of the warm sauce around the edges of the plate and garnish with 4 fried basil leaves.

Red Drum

803 Coleman Boulevard, Mount Pleasant
(843) 849-0313
reddrumrestaurant.com
Chef/Owner: Ben Berryhill

"The intersection of South by Southwest" is how chef and owner Ben Berryhill describes both himself and the food he prepares at Red Drum, a warm, winning Southwestern standout. The Houston native spent summers on his grandparents' east Texas working farm, cooking huge spreads of ham, beans, biscuits, and cornbread for the farmhands with his "country cook" grandmother, and winters working through recipes with his "cookbook chef" mom.

Ben's professional career began with cooking at pizza joints in Hawaii, but it reached its pre–Red Drum pinnacle while Ben was working with Robert Del Grande at Cafe Annie in Houston. It was there that the Culinary Institute of America grad drank in the subtle, analytic culinary approach of Del Grande, whom Ben calls "a founding father of Southwestern cooking."

Ben is without question Charleston's founding father of Southwestern cuisine. Prior to his restaurant's opening in 2005, there was a total dearth of the piquant stuff here. Red Drum—a name for a local fish—brings it on big time, in dishes like wood-grilled barbecue-bathed Lowcountry shrimp paired with sweet corn pudding and a green chile butter sauce. The mood is always convivial here. The bar bounces with what Ben calls "local *Cheers* feel," while the spacious dining room is soothed by the snap-crackle-pop of real wood fires, hulking beams brought in from a farm in North Carolina, and locally crafted ironwork.

This salmon dish is representative of Ben's mission to use indigenous ingredients stamped with signature Southwestern style. He shared this—the recipe for the most popular dish at Red Drum—exclusively for this book. The corn pudding is probably one of the best things you'll ever put in your mouth.

WOOD-GRILLED SALMON WITH RED PEPPER PUREE AND SWEET CORN PUDDING

(SERVES 6)

For the red pepper puree:

4 red bell peppers
2 tablespoons olive oil
1 carrot, peeled and coarsely chopped
1 small onion, coarsely chopped
4 cloves garlic, coarsely chopped
2 red jalapeños, seeded and chopped
Salt and freshly ground black pepper to taste
¼ cup white wine
2 cups chicken stock
⅛ cup heavy cream

For the corn pudding:

24 ears fresh corn, shucked

1 stick (¼ pound) cold unsalted butter, cut into 8 tablespoon-sized pieces

2 shallots, finely minced

¾ cup heavy cream

Salt and freshly ground black pepper to taste

For the salmon:

1 pound hickory or oak wood chips

6 6-ounce salmon fillets, skin removed

Salt and freshly ground black pepper to taste

½ cup melted butter

To prepare the red pepper puree, begin by roasting the red bell peppers (see page 86). In a medium pot, heat the olive oil over medium heat. Add the carrot, onion, garlic, and jalapeños, season lightly with salt and pepper, and stir until the vegetables have softened, about 5 minutes. Deglaze the pot with the white wine and cook over medium-high heat until the wine is reduced by half, about 1 minute. Add the chicken stock and simmer over low heat for 25 minutes. Add the heavy cream and roasted red peppers and simmer for 10 more minutes. Remove pot from the stove and cool. Puree in a blender or food processor until smooth. Return puree to a medium saucepan, taste, and adjust salt and pepper as needed. Add cream to finish. Set puree aside. (Note: The puree can be made 2–3 days in advance, but don't add the cream until just before serving.)

To prepare the corn pudding, preheat the oven to 350°F. Grate the corn with a large box grater, using the medium or large holes, into a 2-quart, ovenproof casserole dish. (This process helps extract the essential juices from the corn. The cobs should be dry, but do not cut too deeply into the hard part of the cob.) This will yield about 6 cups of grated corn. Cover the casserole tightly with foil and bake for 25 minutes. Remove foil, stir to move any corn that is dry or starting to brown away from the edges, and cook uncovered for an additional 10–15 minutes. Remove the casserole from the oven and cool slightly. The corn should look like a semi-dry corn paste.

Heat a large sauté pan over medium to medium-high heat. Add 2 tablespoons of the butter and the minced shallots, stirring. Cook, sweating the shallots until translucent, about 5 minutes. Add the heavy cream and increase the heat to high, bringing the mixture to a boil. Add the corn and season to taste with salt and pepper. When the corn starts to bubble, remove from the heat and gradually stir in the remaining butter, until just melted. Keep warm over a double boiler or gentle water bath until ready to serve.

To prepare the salmon, soak the wood chips for about 2 hours before grilling. Heat a gas or charcoal grill to medium hot. Drain the soaked chips and scatter over the hot coals, or place the damp wood chips on a roasting sheet off to the side of the grill if you're cooking over gas. Season the salmon with salt and freshly ground black pepper. Brush the fillets with the melted butter on both sides to prevent sticking. Place the salmon on the grill and cover. Cook for about 3 minutes (depending on thickness and desired doneness) on the first side and turn, repeating on the second side, keeping the grill covered.

To serve, reheat the red pepper puree. Place a pool of the corn pudding in the center of each plate. Top with a fillet of salmon. Spoon some of the puree all around the center of the plate.

Anson Restaurant

12 Anson Street, downtown
(843) 577-0551
ansonrestaurant.com
Executive Chef: Jeremy Holst

Pretty in pink, wrought iron, and delicate French doors, Anson recalls the look and feel of New Orleans's French Quarter, but she is 100 percent Lowcountry. The old gal's been around for a long time (since 1992!), but in executive chef Jeremy Holst's hands, her cuisine tastes as fresh as ever.

Bacon is cured in-house and shrimp stock is prepared from local shrimp. Whole dried corn grown in South Carolina is delivered and ground in the restaurant's very own stone gristmill, which separates the ground corn into grits, cornmeal, and polenta. These are used handily in dishes like cornmeal-dusted okra, cornmeal-fried okra, and, of course, this memorable interpretation of shrimp and grits, which marries the round mouthfeel of braised pork belly with sweet local shrimp. (Ask your butcher a few days in advance to cut and reserve the pork belly.)

ANSON'S GRITS WITH SHRIMP AND BRAISED BACON

(SERVES 6)

For the braised bacon:

1 teaspoon fennel seed
1 teaspoon coriander seed
1 teaspoon cumin seed
Pinch of red pepper flakes
½ teaspoon whole black peppercorns
1 whole star anise
⅛ teaspoon cloves
⅛ teaspoon whole allspice
1 tablespoon salt
1 tablespoon brown sugar
2 pounds fresh pork belly
1 tablespoon olive oil
½ onion
½ carrot, peeled
1 stalk celery
Sodium-free chicken stock or water to cover
2–3 sprigs fresh thyme
1–2 bay leaves

For the grits:

6 cups water
2 cups stone-ground grits
1 cup heavy cream
3 tablespoons unsalted butter
Salt and freshly ground black pepper to taste

For the shrimp stock:

1 tablespoon vegetable oil
1 quart raw shrimp shells
½ cup onion, finely diced
1 small carrot, peeled and finely diced
1 stalk celery, finely diced
1 teaspoon fennel seed
4 whole black peppercorns
1 bay leaf
3 sprigs fresh thyme

5 parsley stems

2 tablespoons tomato paste

¼ cup dry white wine

For the sauce and to finish:

2 pounds vine-ripe tomatoes

1½–2 pounds large (21–25 count) shrimp, peeled and deveined

Salt and freshly ground black pepper to taste

2 tablespoons butter

6–8 scallions, thinly sliced

Prepare the spice rub and marinate the pork belly up to 3 days ahead. Place the fennel seed, coriander seed, cumin seed, red pepper flakes, peppercorns, whole star anise, cloves, and whole allspice in a medium skillet preheated over medium-high heat. Toast, tossing, until the spices release their aromas and take on a light color, about 2 minutes. Remove from the pan and grind in a spice grinder or small food processor. Transfer spices to a small bowl and combine with the salt and brown sugar. Rub the mixture evenly into all sides of the pork belly. Place the belly in an ovenproof casserole dish and cover tightly with plastic wrap. Refrigerate overnight or for up to 2 days.

Preheat the oven to 300°F 4–5 hours before you plan to serve this dish. Heat the olive oil in a small pot over medium heat. Add the onion, carrot, and celery and sauté for about 3 minutes. Add just enough stock or water to cover the vegetables. Add the thyme and bay leaves. Remove the pork belly from the refrigerator and discard the plastic wrap. Pour the vegetables, stock, and herbs over the belly to just cover it. Cover the casserole dish tightly with aluminum foil. Bake for 4–5 hours, or until the pork is easily pierced with a fork. Remove the pork from the liquid and cool. Cut the belly into 1-ounce cubes and set aside, discarding the cooking liquid.

About 2 hours before serving, prepare the grits. Bring the water to a boil in a medium saucepan. Add the grits and whisk thoroughly to combine. Reduce the heat to low and cook for 1 hour or until the grits are tender, stirring very frequently with a flat-tipped wooden spatula. You may need to add a little extra water if they seem too thick. Once the grits are tender and the water is absorbed, add the cream and butter and stir to combine. Season to taste with salt and pepper. Keep the grits warm over low heat or a water bath for up to 2 hours, adding more cream if needed.

Meanwhile, prepare the shrimp stock. In a medium pot, heat the vegetable oil over high heat. When very hot, add the shrimp shells. (Use the shells from the shrimp for the sauce or ask your fishmonger for some. Whenever you have shrimp shells, you can freeze them for future use in stocks like this one.) Sear the shrimp shells, stirring occasionally, until the shells turn bright pink. Reduce the heat to low, add the vegetables, spices, and herbs. Continue to cook, stirring, for 3–4 more minutes. Add the tomato paste, stirring to combine, and cook another 2 minutes. Add the wine, stir, and cook down to a glaze. Add water—just enough to cover the shells—bring up to a simmer over medium-high heat, and cook for 30 minutes. Strain stock through a fine-mesh sieve or chinois. Return the stock to the same pot. Turn the heat up to high and reduce the stock by half. Skim any fat or impurities that rise to the surface, strain once again, and set aside. (The stock stores very well frozen in an airtight container for several months.)

To make the sauce and complete the dish, preheat the broiler. Cut the tomatoes in half horizontally and place cut side down on a baking sheet. Place the sheet under the broiler and broil until the tomato skins are slightly charred and pulling away from the fruit. Cool the tomatoes and remove and discard skin. Finely chop the tomatoes and set aside.

Preheat the oven to 375°F. Place 18 small bacon slabs fat side down in a single layer in a large ovenproof sauté pan. Place the pan in the oven and bake until crisped, about 15 minutes. Remove the bacon and keep warm on a foil-covered plate. Drain off all but 1 tablespoon of the bacon fat and heat the pan over medium-high heat. Add the shrimp and season with salt and pepper. Toss once or twice. When the shrimp are just turning opaque, after about 1½ minutes, add the tomatoes and toss. Add the shrimp stock, increase heat to high, and bring to a simmer. Add the butter and scallions, stirring to blend. Reduce heat to low until ready to serve.

To serve, spoon 1–1¼ cups of grits into six shallow bowls and scatter with bacon. Top each with the shrimp and tomato sauce. Serve immediately. This dish can also be served from a large platter.

OLD VILLAGE POST HOUSE INN

101 Pitt Street, Mount Pleasant
(843) 388-8935
oldvillageposthouseinn.com
Executive Chef: Antonia Krenza

On a quiet street in the heart of Mount Pleasant's Mayberry-esque Old Village, a few doors down from a retro pharmacy that serves milkshakes and grilled cheese sandwiches at the counter, resides the Old Village Post House. A functioning inn with six guest rooms, the charming old house was originally an overnight stop for nineteenth-century horseback-riding mailmen. The Post House just oozes neighborhood charm and looks the inviting part with Old-World bead board, soft earthy colors, and silent paddle fans working their meditative magic overhead.

This stunningly delicious take on shrimp and grits (created by former chef de cuisine Jim Walker) includes country ham, Cajun seasoning, and andouille sausage. Even though he's no longer at the restaurant (former sous chef Antonia Krenza was recently promoted to executive chef talent), I decided to leave it in the new edition because it is such a remarkable version of shrimp and grits and relatively easy to make at home.

LOWCOUNTRY SHRIMP AND GRITS

(SERVES 4–6)

For the grits:

8 cups water

3 cups stone-ground grits

1 stick (¼ pound) unsalted butter

1–1½ cups heavy cream

Sea or kosher salt and freshly ground black pepper to taste

For the shrimp sauce:

2 tablespoons vegetable oil

1¾ pounds Thibodeaux's andouille sausage (or substitute another brand), cut into approximately 28 ½-inch-thick slices

1 cup cubed country ham (cut into ¼-inch dice)

1¼ pounds large (21–25 count) shrimp, peeled and deveined

½ cup peeled and seeded tomatoes, finely chopped

¼ cup scallions, finely sliced

4 teaspoons garlic, minced

4 teaspoons Cajun-style fish blackening seasoning (suggest R.L. Schreiber brand)

1 cup salt-free chicken stock

4 tablespoons unsalted butter

Sea or kosher salt and freshly ground black pepper to taste

To prepare the grits, bring the water to a boil over high heat in a large heavy-bottomed pot. Add the grits, stir, and bring back to a boil, stirring constantly with a whisk or flat-tipped wooden spoon to prevent sticking. Continue cooking on low heat, stirring, until thickened (the grits should plop like a thick cornbread batter), 30–40 minutes. Turn off the burner and let stand covered, so that the grits can continue to slowly absorb the water, for 1–2 hours.

Just before serving, reheat the grits over medium heat, stirring for about 5 minutes. Add the butter and the heavy cream, stirring to incorporate. Heat through and season to taste with salt and pepper.

Meanwhile, about 20 minutes before serving, prepare the shrimp sauce. Heat the oil over high heat in a large deep sauté pan. When hot and sizzling, add the sausage and country ham. Sauté, tossing until the sausage and ham begin to turn golden and caramelize, about 5 minutes. Reduce the heat to medium-high. Add the shrimp, tomato, scallions, minced garlic, and Cajun-style fish blackening seasoning. Sauté for another 3 minutes, being sure to combine well and coat the ingredients evenly with the seasoning. Add the chicken stock, increase the heat to high, and cook for 1 minute. Stir in the butter and cook until the shrimp are cooked through, another 1–2 minutes. Season to taste with salt and pepper.

To serve, ladle the grits into shallow bowls and top with the sauce. Serve immediately.

Toast of Charleston

155 Meeting Street, downtown
843-534-0043
toastofcharleston.com
Kitchen Manager: Billie Littles

As a child growing up in Statesboro, Georgia under the strict and loving tutelage of her grandfather (who served as a cook in the military), Billie Littles was taught to cook to be "independent, nurture and maintain herself."

The only girl out of a family of four, she took her grandfather's advice to heart starting out first in hotel management and later in restaurants. She's been at the heart of the kitchen at Toast's downtown location (there are also sister restaurants in nearby West Ashley and Summerville) for more than a decade.

Her version of the restaurant's signature Toast Étouffée is a minimally retouched version of the recipe created by the restaurant that previously occupied the same space—a Southern-inspired, everybody knows your name kind of space that served breakfast, lunch, and dinner.

Almost everyone says this, but when Billie says it, with her even, low voice and soft brown eyes, you really believe it: "The key is preparing it (all food) with love." She plates the chunky, shrimp étouffée "gravy" served over creamy grits with fried green tomatoes down the middle and three large, fresh shrimp diced and quickly cooked into the finished étouffée.

© Stan Jernigan-The Digital Eye

TOAST ÉTOUFFÉE

(SERVES 6– 8)

2 sticks (1 cup) unsalted butter
1 cup yellow onion, finely chopped
1 cup celery, finely chopped
1 cup green pepper, seeded and finely chopped
½ cup fresh carrots, finely diced and peeled
1 cup all-purpose flour
1½ teaspoons prepared shrimp demi-glace
4 cups water
4 cups tomato juice
½ cup heavy whipping cream
½ cup fresh tomato, seeded and finely diced
2 teaspoons dried basil leaves
2 teaspoons dried thyme leaves
½ teaspoon Hot Texas Pete Sauce
Kosher salt to taste
Ground White Pepper to taste
½ pound (about 1 cup) fresh shrimp, peeled and coarsely chopped

Melt the butter in a large pot over medium heat. Add the onion, celery, pepper, and carrots. Cook until just softened, stirring, about 5 minutes. Stir in the flour all at once and blend thoroughly with wooden spoon. Cook about five minutes until the flour has just started to turn a light caramel color. Combine the shrimp demi-glace with the water in a large bowl and whisk to combine. Stir the mixture into the pot. Add the tomato juice and bring up to a boil over high heat. Reduce to a simmer. Add the remaining ingredients (except the shrimp), stir and simmer gently for 10 minutes. Taste and adjust seasoning as needed. Add the shrimp and cook until just pink, about 1 minute. Serve immediately over grits (see page 139 for how to prepare grits).

The Ordinary

544 King Street, downtown
(843) 414-7060
eattheordinary.com
Chef/Owner: Mike Lata

James Beard Award-winning chef Mike Lata, who owns both FIG (which stands for "food is good" which should really be "great;" see FIG, page 38) and this humbly named, elegant oyster house, has an affinity for pure understatement in his restaurant's names and what's served on their plates. Although the "understatement" in his streamlined technique, precision sourcing, and minimalist cooking style ends up consistently making standing ovation worthy statements.

When Lata set up shop in this elegant old bank building (complete with a working vault), he actually had pig on the brain. "With all of the attention that pigs were getting in the first decade of the century, I thought there was room for a new conversation about seafood. It seemed to me that we could create a restaurant that showcased a real sense of place through seafood. I first started thinking about this in 2007. We opened the doors in 2012," says Lata.

As for the name, well, it goes back to shrimpers, crabbers and fishermen. "We are celebrating the relationships we've created with them. The Ordinary is a shrine and temple for them to showcase their products. We came across the name in an old book about oysters. There was a seafood restaurant in Manhattan a long time ago called Holtz Ordinary. We learned that it comes from an Old English term for a kind of public eating house. It had such a great ring to it and captured what we wanted to create: a public gathering place that celebrated local seafood."

As for oysters, there are always two local oyster and four more, almost always from the East Coast and different parts of the Atlantic, including Nova Scotia, Maine, and Massachusetts. "We serve all East Coast oysters because we want guests to be able to experience the way that the climate and unique conditions of each place can influence the flavor and texture of the oyster (what we call the "merroir," like the "terroir" of a wine)," says Lata.

Lata's fish schnitzel represents the kinds of dishes he prepares at the restaurant, what he calls "quick cooking and speedy, but also a different way to approach cooking fish." It's a departure from the normal fish fillet entree that you find at many restaurants. "This is typically something that you would do with meat, but we found that it works beautifully with several species of fish," says Lata.

Insider tip: while you're here, don't miss the house-made Hawaiian rolls and warm, chunky lobster rolls. Chef Lata recommends serving this schnitzel with a fresh, simple green salad, similar to the arugula salad executive chef Jason Stanhope shared at sister restaurant FIG (also owned by Lata) on page 38.

FISH SCHNITZEL

(SERVES 4)

1 pound (about 2 cups) sunchokes (also called Jerusalem artichokes), cut into 1-inch pieces

Generous sprinkle sea salt and freshly ground black pepper

5 tablespoons olive oil, divided

Sea salt, to taste

4 5-ounce triggerfish fillets, about 1-inch thick (can substitute any meaty fish such as swordfish, amberjack, grouper)

3 eggs, lightly beaten

1 tablespoon Dijon mustard

2 cups all-purpose flour

2 cups finely ground breadcrumbs (or panko)

2 tablespoons unsalted butter

1 tablespoon capers

3 Meyer lemons, zest finely grated and fruit cut into segments

1 tablespoon finely chopped parsley

Preheat oven to 400°F. Toss sunchokes with 1 tablespoon of olive oil and season with salt and pepper. Spread in a single layer on a baking sheet and roast until browned and tender, about 20 minutes. Set aside.

Put a fish fillet in a large zip top bag and lay it on a flat surface. Using the flat side of a meat mallet or a rolling pin, gently and evenly pound fillet until about ½-inch thick. Remove from bag and repeat with remaining fillets. Season with salt on both sides.

Set up your dredging station. In a medium bowl, whisk together eggs and mustard. Pour flour into a second bowl and breadcrumbs into a third. One at a time, dredge fish fillet in flour, then in egg mixture, and finally in breadcrumbs to coat (shake off excess). Set breaded fish aside and repeat with remaining fish. Season once again with salt.

Heat remaining oil in a large skillet over medium-high heat. Once hot, pan-fry the fillets, two at a time, until golden and crisp, about 3 minutes per side. Transfer to warm serving plates while you complete remaining fillets.

Discard half of the oil remaining in the frying pan and return pan to medium heat. Add butter and melt until sizzling and golden, about 2 minutes. Add capers, lemon zest and segments, roasted sunchokes and parsley to the pan, stirring to coat. Cook until butter smells nutty and darkens slightly, about 2 minutes. Spoon sunchoke mixture and sauce over warm schnitzel. Sprinkle with salt to taste.

Zero Restaurant + Bar

0 George Street, downtown
(843) 817-7900
zerorestaurantcharleston.com
Executive Chef: Vinson Petrillo

When Executive Chef Vinson Petrillo began working at Zero George (which also doubles as a stunning boutique inn *Conde Nast* deemed one of the Top 5 Foodie Hotels in the world), his job was to lead the transition of the hotel cafe into a full-blown restaurant. And, along the way, to lead the intimate cooking classes at the early nineteenth-century property's cooking school. Not surprisingly, Petrillo views both the restaurant and the classes more as a dining experience, and less of a lesson. "I use 'behind the scenes technique' where flavor is the most important thing. Food needs to be delicious, not weird," says Petrillo.

The New Jersey native and Johnson & Wales grad worked his way through a lot of kitchens working only with the best chefs who expected nothing less than perfection. He employs classic French technique, modern, and "new texture" in his unpretentious but utterly pristine creations on the restaurant's three tasting menus: Omnivore, Herbivore, and Pre-Theatre, all paired with corresponding libations.

"There is more to Charleston than shrimp and grits and crab cakes. What I love about doing the tasting menus is it's a way to showcase myriad techniques and flavors in one sitting. Unlike, going to a really great steak place and having 100 bites of steak, you get 100+ bites of a really great assortment," says Petrillo. "But, do I believe my food has to be all local? Absolutely not! That would be like cooking in Italy and only using ingredients from Sicily. It's important to be smart about where you source and find the best ingredients from all over the world."

The chef, who fondly recalls cooking with his hardworking father and family on Sundays, ultimately wants to keep the cooking simple and highlight the best of each ingredient. "It takes a

long time to be able to call yourself a chef. It took me a long time to figure it out; to find out who I am (as a chef) and be able to make what I'm cooking as my very own."

The pan roasted snapper is a luscious example of how Petrillo does just that. "The sauce really makes the dish. We use the heads and the shells and the entire crawfish to make the sauce," he says. From there, he builds the plate with some of the belles of the spring ball: chanterelles, sweet onions, and a revolving door of "spring things," depending on what fresh beauties arrive in his kitchen that day.

A few notes on some of the less commonly found ingredients in this recipe. Beech mushrooms are small white or light brown mushrooms, native to East Asia. If you can't find them, substitute oyster mushrooms. Sea beans, known as samphire in Britain and also called sea asparagus, grow in salt marshes, on beaches, and in mangroves. If you can't find them, use asparagus or green beans. Finally, Cipollini are flat, pale yellow and slightly sweet onions. If you can't find them, use pearl onions instead. Both are challenging to peel. The job becomes much easier if you soak them in hot water for 30 minutes prior to peeling. Making the nage and prepping the vegetables a day or two ahead makes putting this dish together at the last minute a snap!

PAN ROASTED SNAPPER WITH CHANTERELLES, "SPRING THINGS," AND CRAWFISH NAGE

(SERVES 8)

For the crawfish nage:

5 pounds fresh crawfish

¼ cup olive oil

10 cloves garlic, peeled

1 cup onions, diced

1 cup celery, diced

1 cup carrots, diced

¼ cup fresh ginger, diced

4 stalks lemongrass, coarsely chopped

1 bulb fennel, thinly sliced

2 tablespoons toasted fennel seeds

2 tablespoons coriander seeds

1 teaspoon red chili flakes

1 6-ounce can tomato paste

1 cup Pernod (or substitute another licorice liqueur)

1 (750 ml) bottle of good quality white wine

Sea salt or kosher salt to taste

1 cup cold, unsalted butter, cut into ¼-inch dice

Put a large pot of salted water (use about ¼ cup sea salt or kosher salt) on high and bring to a boil. Cook the crawfish, in batches of 10–15, for 1 minute. Drain and immerse immediately in ice water. Remove from the ice water, set aside, and repeat in batches until all of the crawfish are cooked. Separate the heads from the tails. Remove the meat from the tails (it helps to cut through the underside of the shell with scissors, reserve the tail meat and the heads, separately.

In a large sauce pan on medium heat, add the olive oil. Once the olive oil is hot, add the reserved crawfish heads and allow them to develop color and flavor, stirring for 10 minutes. Using a French rolling pin or a long blunt object, smash all the shells until they are completely broken up. Add the garlic, onions, celery, carrots, ginger, lemongrass, fresh fennel, fennel seed, coriander, and red chili flakes. Stir for 5-10 minutes, until the onions become translucent. Using a wooden spatula stir in the tomato paste, and allow it to caramelize over the vegetables, shells, and bottom of the pot. Continue stirring

and scraping the bottom of the pot for 5 minutes. Deglaze the pot with the Pernod and reduce by half. Add the white wine and reduce by half. Then, add just enough tap water to cover all the shells and simmer until reduced by half. Once reduced by half, strain all the liquid through a fine sieve or chinois into another pot and press down on the shells to get out as much flavor as possible. Bring the liquid back up to a simmer and slowly stir in the cold butter until emulsified. Season to taste with salt and reserve warm for serving.

For the "Spring Things":

1 cup fava beans, shucked

1 cup fresh peas, shucked

1 cup Beech mushrooms

1 cup sea beans

2 cups water

2 cups granulated sugar

2 cups white wine vinegar

2 cups chanterelle mushrooms, cleaned

1 cup peeled Cipollini onions, peeled

¼ cup (4 tablespoons) unsalted butter

Juice of 1 lemon

3 tablespoons fresh tarragon, chopped

Sea salt or kosher salt to taste

Bring a large sauce pan to a boil with heavily salted water (using about ¼ cup sea salt or kosher salt). Blanch the fava beans until tender about 3-4 minutes, drain, and shock (submerge) in an ice bath. Repeat the same procedure with the fresh peas. Peel the skin off the fava beans and reserve with the peas. Cut the tops off the Beech mushrooms and place them in a heat-proof container. Place the sea beans in a separate heat-proof container. Bring the sugar, water and vinegar to a boil and cover both the mushrooms and the sea beans to quickly pickle them. Cover both and let cool in the refrigerator until ready to use. (Note: These will store nicely, refrigerated and covered, for several days.)

Cut the chanterelles into bite-size pieces and reserve. Halve the Cipollini onions and then slice them into ¼-inch slices. In a large pan on medium heat add the butter, onions, and chanterelles with a pinch of salt to draw out the moisture and cook slowly in their natural juices. Once onions are tender, about 5 minutes, fold in the peas and fava beans and warm through. Once the peas and fava are warm, add 1 cup of the crawfish nage to the pan and simmer for 1 minute. Gently add the reserved crawfish tail meat and warm through. Finish with a generous squeeze of fresh lemon juice, fresh tarragon, and salt to taste. Reserve warm until the fish is cooked.

For the fish:

8 5-ounce portions of snapper fillets, skin-on

½ cup unsalted butter

Grapeseed oil

8 cloves garlic, peeled

1 bunch fresh thyme

Sea salt to taste

Kosher salt to season fish

Preheat oven to 475°F. Place two large sauté pans on high heat. Season both sides of the fish fillets with kosher salt and coat the bottom of both pans with just enough oil to cover the surface of the bottom of each pan. Once the oil begins to lightly smoke, add 4 pieces of fish to each pan, skin-side down. Press the fish down gently with a spatula to allow for even crispness of the fish. After 1 minute on the stove, transfer to the oven without flipping the fish. Cook the fish in the oven for 6 minutes. Take the fish out of the oven and without any more heat flip the fish so the skin is facing you. Split the butter, garlic and thyme and place on top of the warm fish in both pans. Allow the fish to rest for 5-6 minutes in the butter and herbs.

Divide the warm chanterelle and crawfish mixture evenly between eight dinner plates. Spoon the warm sauce over the plated mixture on each dish. Place 3 pickled sea beans and 3 pickled Beech mushrooms on top of the chanterelle mixture. Place the fish on top and garnish with edible spring leaves or a bit of fresh herbs, such as chopped chives. Serve immediately.

CHEZ NOUS

6 Payne Street, downtown
(843) 579-3060
cheznouschs.com
Co-Owners: Patrick and Franny Panella
Co-Owner/Executive Chef: Jill Mathias

The family that works together stays together. That's times two at this adorable button of an antique wooden-sided house turned formidable French restaurant in 2014. Husband and wife owners Patrick and Franny Panella and executive chef Jill Mathias and her husband Juan (he also works as sous chef) are all partners in the business and in the kitchen. The team met every Thursday for a year before opening the restaurant, hashing out every last detail, from the tables and the chairs right down to how they were going to cut the bread. "I would cook a menu every Thursday and Patrick, Franny (who happens to be French), Juan, and I would write our honest answers on cards asking would you come back for this, etc?" Mathias recalls fondly.

Out of those fifty-two Thursdays together, Mathias was able to come up with a book of 1,200 superb recipes reflecting the restaurant's Southern France, Northern Italy, and Northern Spain culinary roots. Each day, Franny writes out the daily menu which includes two choices each for appetizers, entrees, and desserts, for both lunch and dinner. Mathias works with what's fresh and in her kitchen that day, but the "book" is always there as a guide and reminder. The whole service staff tastes the menu before a single plate goes out, to ensure perfection and familiarity with each ingredient and plate. "Because we are so small, it puts more pressure on us to make the dishes delicious and perfect every single time. And either Franny or Patrick is always in-house, so there is a real sense of continuity and family."

Mathias, a Johnson & Wales grad, favors simple, rustic, and homey food. Fish is one of her favorite things to work with because we have such a vast and wonderfully fresh selection available from local waters, and also because it's widely used in Mediterranean cooking. "The olive oil poached snapper is so simple and easy for the home cook. We usually use snapper because it looks so beautiful and clean and pair it with whatever vegetables are in season, often turnips, baby carrots and spring onions." However, the olive oil poaching method works for many different types of fish. Feel free to substitute for the freshest you can find. However, very frail thin fillets, such as flounder, may not be a suitable choice.

OLIVE OIL POACHED SNAPPER WITH PEARL ONIONS, BABY CARROTS, AND BABY TURNIPS

(SERVES 4)

16 pearl onions, peeled
20 baby carrots, peeled and halved
20 baby turnips, peeled and halved
3 tablespoons kosher or sea salt
6 bay leaves
30 peppercorns

3 sprigs fresh thyme

4 5-ounce snapper fillet with skin

1 cup olive oil

1 tablespoon unsalted butter

¼ cup water

1 tablespoon unsalted butter

1 tablespoon fresh parsley, finely chopped

Juice of 1 lemon

Pinch sea salt

Pre-heat oven to 350°F. In three separate, medium sized sauté pans, place onions, carrots, and turnips with 1 tablespoon each of salt, 2 bay leaves, 1 sprig thyme, and 10 peppercorns. Place enough water in each pan to just cover the vegetables. Bring up to a simmer over medium heat and simmer until tender. Strain the vegetables and set aside. Discard water and herbs. (Note: You can prep the vegetables up to this point a day ahead and store, refrigerated, in sealed containers.)

Put the olive oil in a large, oven proof pan. Arrange the fish in a single layer, skin-side down. Place in the oven and cook for 6 minutes. Baste the fish with the oil, and continue to cook until fish is opaque and cooked through, about 10 minutes.

Place all vegetables in a large pan with ¼ cup water. Bring up to a simmer over medium heat. When the water has reduced by half, add the butter and cook until the water is reduced further and the vegetables are glossy. Add chopped parsley and stir to coat. Divide vegetables among 4 plates. Top each with 1 poached fish fillet, skin-side up. Sprinkle with sea salt and a squeeze of lemon.

HIGH THYME

2213 Middle Street, Sullivan's Island
(843) 883-3536
highthymecuisine.com
Chef/Co-owner: Taylor Still

Named after the herb and with a nod towards The Grateful Dead, this familial, neighborhood favorite has been part of the Sullivan's Island restaurant scene far longer than most of its neighbors, dating back to 2003. A good bit of credit for its popularity and enduring appeal has to go to chef/co-owner Taylor Still and his front-of-the-house "work spouse" and co-owner, Emily Daniels.

With just fourty-five covers, not counting the petite outside porch, and a breezy, beachfront address, Chef Still says their biggest customer base is locals and island regulars. "It's a relationship between me and Emily and the people in the front. I like to keep the food accessible but interesting. We're feeding peoples' families."

Formerly a psychology major at the College of Charleston, Still found himself increasingly drawn towards professional cooking. He worked in several local kitchens before setting up shop at High Thyme. "It was a blessing and a curse. It was wonderful to be on my own, but I had to give up the corporate guidance and support I [had] had in previous kitchens, such as Blossom and Anson (see page 135)," Still says.

Chef Still favors the "big strong flavors" of the Mediterranean, and frequently employs them in his 60 percent seafood intensive menu, in addition to daily specials and in-demand favorites such as lasagna Bolognese and fried lentil cakes.

For the scallop dish, Chef Still uses "U/10" scallops which is another way of saying they're really, really big, as in it takes fewer than 10 to equal 1 pound. Another term for these size scallops is jumbo scallops or sea scallops. Ask your fishmonger to help you find the right fit.

PAN-SEARED SCALLOPS WITH COUNTRY HAM CREAM, SHAVED BEETS AND PICKLED CABBAGE

(SERVES 4)

1 head purple cabbage, shredded

2 tablespoons olive oil

2 tablespoons rice wine vinegar

8 scallops, dry pak U/10, clean and dry

2 large golden beets, poached, peeled, and thinly sliced

½ cup country ham, sliced and julienned

2 tablespoons shallot, mini-diced

½ cup brandy

1 cup heavy cream

Salt and pepper

Preheat oven to 500°F.

Toss the shredded purple cabbage in 1 tablespoon of olive oil, rice wine vinegar, and season with salt and pepper. Roast on an ungreased cookie sheet for 5 minutes. Put aside for garnish.

Season scallops generously with salt and pepper. Heat a heavy bottom or cast iron skillet over medium-high heat with 1 tablespoon of oil until nearly smoking, 1–2 minutes. Sear scallops, approximately 3–4 minutes per side. Remove from pan and set aside.

Add country ham and shallots to the pan and deglaze with brandy. Add cream and reduce by half.

To serve, place an equal number of beet slices on 4 plates. Place 2 scallops onto each plate. Spoon the brandy cream over the scallops. Garnish with pickled cabbage on top. Serve immediately and enjoy.

Coda del Pesce

1130 Ocean Boulevard, Isle of Palms
(843) 242-8570
codadelpesce.com
Owner/Executive Chef/Sommelier: Ken Vedrinski

Highly-lauded Executive Chef/Owner Ken Vedrinski (who also owns and runs the kitchen at downtown's Trattoria Lucca (page 104), wasn't sure about opening a second restaurant, until a friend showed him the space that now houses Coda del Pesce ("tail of the fish" in Italian). Dramatic, up-close views of the Atlantic reminded him of his family's town near the Adriatic Sea and a seaside restaurant he frequented about 45 minutes from there. "It was very stylish. They had a mix of sophistication, linens on tables near the beach, and just brilliant food and seafood. I said that if I can do this with Lucca, an old classic, I can do this with a water view that's still casual and elegant," explains Vedrinski.

So, Coda del Pesce was born in 2013 and has been a favorite seafood destination for casual elegance with a view ever since. "I like to cook relevant, consistently delicious food. We look for alternative stuff that we like, and then write it into the menu every day. For example, I recently came across some local conch from stone crabs. Nobody's using them. We make a beautiful Bolognese from them." Serving almost 80 percent seafood dishes, Vedrinski uses 100 percent local seafood and pays fisherman in cash to ensure priority freshness and availability.

Chef Vedrinski uses swordfish from nearby Wadmalaw Island's celebrated Cherry Point Seafood to prepare his breaded and fried fish picatta served with a spicy lemon and tomato sauce. Use the absolute freshest you can find.

Simple and beautiful, he calls the sauce a "5 minute marinara." Lemon Agrumato is a cold-extracted extra virgin olive oil pressed with whole lemons and olives to produce this super aromatic and flavorful oil that is the base of the pungent sauce. You can find it in specialty shops or online. A Calabrese chili is a small, red, ultra-piquant chili grown in Calabria, Italy. Chef Vedrinski suggests a jalapeno pepper substitute, but there is no substituting using a microplane to grate the Parmesan Reggiano. It's crucial for the fluffy texture of the fish breading. This comes together very fast. Have everything out and measured before you get started.

PICATTA OF CHERRY POINT SWORDFISH "TORCINO STYLE"

(SERVES 4)

3 cloves garlic, thinly sliced

¼ cup Lemon Agrumato extra virgin olive oil

1 Calabrese chili, finely chopped (or substitute ½ jalapeno pepper, seeded and finely chopped)

1 1-pound heirloom tomato, peeled and seeded (about 1½ cups)

Sea salt or kosher salt lightly to taste

For the fish:

4 5-ounce swordfish steaks, cut ½-inch thick

Sea salt or kosher salt and freshly ground black pepper to taste

½–¾ cup all-purpose flour for dusting the fish

1 whole egg

3 egg whites

½ cup best quality Parmesan Reggiano, grated finely on a microplane

½ cup finely chopped fresh parsley

¼ cup chopped basil

⅓ cup olive oil

Sauté the garlic in Lemon Agrumato in a medium saucepan over medium low heat until softened. Do not color. Add the chopped chili/pepper and chopped tomato, and cook through until the chili's just softened and the tomato's warmed through. Season to taste with salt. Cover and keep warm.

Separately, season the swordfish lightly with salt and pepper. Dredge the seasoned fish in the flour and shake off the excess. In a medium bowl, beat together the whole egg and egg whites with a fork or whisk. Mix in the Parmesan, parsley, and basil. Dip the dredged fish into the mixture and shake off excess. Heat the olive oil in a large sauté pan over medium heat. Add the fish in a single layer, well-spaced. Cook about 3 minutes on the first side, or until lightly browned. Gently turn over and repeat on the second side.

To serve, generously portion some of the warm tomato sauce on each plate (or a single platter) and top with the warm swordfish picatta. Serve hot.

PLEASE WAIT TO BE SEATED
RAW BAR
CEVICHE
FISH TACO
PO'BOY
FISH SANDWICH
SPECIALS
AIX
WESTBROOK

167 Raw

289 East Bay Street, downtown
(843) 579-4997
167raw.com
Executive Chef: Mike Geib

167 Raw's owner, Jesse Sandole, is the son of a very successful operator of a Nantucket, Massachusetts based fish market called East Coast Provision. But, Executive Chef Mike Geib (and Sandole's College of Charleston friend) says everyone called it 167 because of the address. Sandole would head to Nantucket in the summers off from college and do a pop-up raw bar right next to the market. It was a huge hit, so Sandole decided to do something similar here in Charleston.

This cosmopolitan chic pocket-of-a-place started out mostly as a fish market serving food. It has since shed its market ways and is a fully-formed restaurant. Geib, who cut his teeth in several prominent kitchens including with cousin Fred Neuville at Fat Hen (page 4), was brought on to help with the transformation. "About sixty percent of the menu was in place. I organized, synchronized and added to the menu, and brought in some local purveyors," Geib says.

Some of the crowd favorites in this no reservations, first-come, first-serve space are crisp oyster baskets, tuna burgers, a butter-toasted chunky lobster roll, and the poke (recipe follows). "Most of our seafood is driven down twice a week from the day boats in Nantucket and we use local seafood for specials. For the best possible results, I feel it is important to take a subtle approach and really let the ingredients shine," says a very enthusiastic Geib.

Chef Geib pairs this refreshing sweet/salty poke (a Hawaiian term and recipe for a raw fish salad) with chips and guacamole over rice. "It's the perfect communal plate and the best way to get people in the mood for what's coming next in their meal."

Ahi Poke

(SERVES 4)

1 cup soy sauce
4 tablespoons light brown sugar
2 teaspoons fresh lime juice
1 teaspoon Sriracha sauce
8 ounces high quality (preferably Number 1 Grade) yellow fin tuna, cut into 1-inch cubes
2 teaspoons fresh cilantro, finely chopped
1 teaspoon sesame seeds (for garnish)

Combine the soy sauce and brown sugar in a small saucepan. Whisk to combine and simmer over high heat until reduced by two-thirds. Set aside to cool. Whisk two tablespoons of the cooled reduction with the lime juice and Sriracha in a medium bowl. Add the tuna and cilantro and toss gently to coat. Refrigerate in a covered container for up to 1 hour. Serve in a bowl or on a platter. Garnish with a drizzle of the sesame seeds.

Beef, Barbecue, Sides, and More

Charleston chefs take meat and potatoes to new heights and go crazy for artisanally-raised livestock from local farmers. McCrady's Sean Brock raises his own pigs, which he lovingly converts into charcuterie. In 2016, once singular McCrady's became two—one part dinner tasting menu at the restaurant and one part tavern history and comfort next door. McCrady's Tavern steak royale features an oyster and bacon infused sauce to complement a sturdy New York Strip. Speaking of bacon, Oak Steakhouse's executive chef, Jeremiah Bacon, braises short ribs long and slow and finishes the sauce with a chunky, sweet puree of root vegetables.

Inside this chapter, you'll sample steak two ways from The Ocean Room and Halls Chophouse. Both chefs provide their own perspective on how to grill the best steak, in addition to a personally-crafted menu for an entire outside grill meal from Halls' Matthew Niessner.

Barbecue, particularly the pig variety, is a long Charleston and South Carolina tradition, but these days expands to Texas with Lewis Barbecue and back home again with Rodney Scott's famous Hemingway, SC BBQ, now settled in Charleston. Pitmasters are notoriously stingy with recipes for meat rubs and sauces, but these gentlemen were happy to share some of their best sides, including John Lewis's Hatch Green Chile Corn Pudding and Scott's plucky, fork-tender collards. Tuck in your napkin and dig in.

McCrady's Restaurant

155 East Bay Street, downtown
mccradysrestaurant.com
Chef/Partner: Sean Brock

McCrady's Tavern

2 Unity Alley, downtown
(843) 577-0025
mccradystavern.com
Chef/Partner: Sean Brock

If job satisfaction plays a prominent role in life expectancy, Sean Brock will live a very, very long time. The 2008 and 2009 James Beard Rising Star Chef nominee and 2010 Best Chef Southeast winner talks about his restaurants (which now include Minero, page 98 and Husk, see page 100), cooking, farming, raising pigs, protein's reaction to heat, heirloom seeds, and house-made charcuterie with the same beaming pride and love with which a father speaks of his child.

And he knows what he's talking about. A staunch proponent of sous vide and slow cooking, he and his staff also tend a biodynamic garden on two-and-a-half acres of land on nearby Wadmalaw Island, from which he culls produce for his restaurants and heirloom seeds to preserve dying breeds. As if that weren't enough, Sean also farms pigs that he converts into bacon, ham, and charcuterie.

"Our garden writes our menu. Spending time out there, hoeing onions, I smell them and all I can think about is how I'm going to cook them later that evening," says Sean with endearing enthusiasm. His combination of razor-sharp classical technique and contemporary whimsy has turned restaurant critics' and patrons' heads across the country.

McCrady's is something of an old soul, situated in what was once a public house (circa 1788) where George Washington came to dinner on a visit to Charleston during the Revolutionary War. The original heart pine floors and softened antique brick edges echo with whispers of the past, even as Brock fixes his gastronomic gaze entirely on the future, making heavenly food that's also kind to the planet.

Brock lovingly shaped McCrady's into two new, dynamic parts in September 2016. McCrady's Restaurant is now an intimate space, seating just 22 happy souls and serving up to 15–18 courses on a menu-only dinner tasting menu. Nearby, at the old

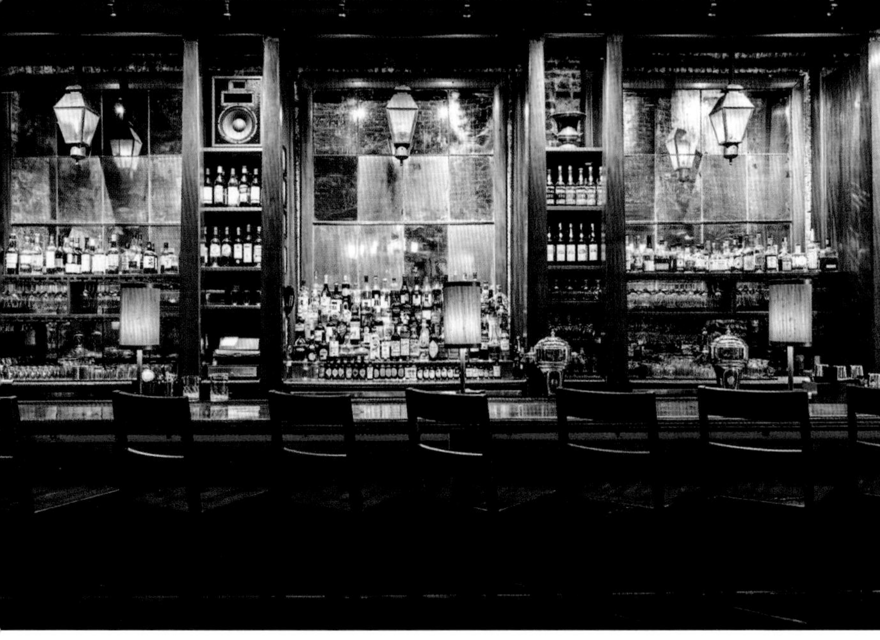

tavern, the menu and the mood are more casual and food and drink are served for brunch, lunch, and dinner. Brock's soul, products, and technique respect the culinary core of the old South, but "reimagined."

Benton's bacon comes from Benton's Smoky Mountain Country Hams curing and smoking outfit in Madisonville, Tennessee. It's been called the world's best bacon for a reason. This is the real, smoky McCoy and it can be purchased online. If you can't get Benton's, find the best quality bacon available. This refined yet gutsy dish is typical of the style of food Brock serves at McCrady's Tavern. This recipe makes enough sauce for 1 or 2 steaks, but the Royale base can be finished as directed to sauce several more.

TAVERN STEAK ROYALE

(SERVES 1-2, WITH EXTRA SAUCE BASE)

For the Royale base:

1 tablespoon unsalted whole butter

1 tablespoon all-purpose flour

1 cup chicken stock

¾ cup heavy cream

1 tablespoon dried oysters or other dried seafood, minced

½ cup oyster liquor

1 teaspoon unsalted whole butter

Red Wine, to taste

To finish the sauce and steak:

1 steak (suggest NY Strip or Ribeye), grilled to your preference

1 tablespoon leeks, cut into diamond shapes

1 tablespoon bacon, cut into large dice or lardons (preferably Benton's bacon)

2 tablespoons Royale base

3-6 freshly shucked oysters, liquor reserved

1 tablespoon peeled, seeded, and finely chopped tomato "concasse," cut into diamond shapes

Fresh lemon juice, to taste

Sea or kosher salt and freshly ground black pepper, to taste

Red wine, to taste

1 tablespooons Fines herbs, finely chopped (equal parts chopped parsley, chive, chervil and tarragon)

Melt butter in a small 1-quart saucepot. Whisk in flour to make a roux. Lightly cook the roux for about 1 minute, try not to add any color. Slowly whisk in the chicken stock, bring to a simmer. Once the stock is beginning to get thick, whisk in the heavy cream and add the dried seafood. Bring to a simmer again and let cook gently for 10-15 minutes, or until the roux is cooked out. Whisk in the oyster liquor at the last minute and strain through a fine mesh sieve. Reserve warm. (Or, prepare a day ahead and store, refrigerated, in a sealed container overnight).

To start, grill the steak to your liking (see The Ocean Room's Chef Bowling's directions for grilling the perfect steak and his grilled New York Strip and béarnaise recipe, page 169). Set aside to rest. While resting, combine the leeks, bacon and Royale base in a small saucepot and bring to a simmer. Once hot, add oysters and tomatoes. Heat just until the outside of the oyster begins to curl. Season with the lemon juice, salt and pepper. At the last-minute, add a dash of the red wine and fines herbs. Whisk in the butter and pour the sauce onto a plate. Slice the steak and lay out across the sauce.

Oak Steakhouse

17 Broad Street, downtown
(843) 722-4220
oaksteakhouserestaurant.com
Executive Chef: Jeremiah Bacon

The hearty, sophisticated steak and Italian fare served at Oak pairs wonderfully with the dreamily beautiful nineteenth-century bank morphed into a dining destination extraordinaire.

The restaurant features a full-service bar on the ground level that highlights the expansive wine program and cocktail menu, then ascends via a grand staircase, past a middle-level dining area, to the butter yellow and muted blue elegance of the top-tier dining room. No matter what the level, USDA Prime Certified Angus Beef, and pristinely purveyed local produce and seafood are Oak's star attractions.

Lowcountry native and Culinary Institute of America grad Jeremiah Bacon spent a decade working in and around New York City, including stints at Le Bernadin and Per Se, before returning home to Charleston. He took over the helm at Oak, a classic American steakhouse serving both wet- and dry-aged beef, in 2010.

Bacon's classical technique and commitment to using the highest grade meat is reflected in this sumptuous yet surprisingly simple feast.

Braised Certified Angus Beef (CAB) Prime Short Ribs with Root Vegetable Mash and Watercress

(SERVES 4–6)

For the short ribs:

4 10-ounce CAB Prime short ribs
1 tablespoon kosher or sea salt
2 teaspoons freshly ground black pepper
⅓ cup vegetable oil, divided
3 carrots, peeled and coarsely chopped
1 celery root, peeled and coarsely chopped
4 celery ribs, coarsely chopped
1 large onion, peeled and coarsely chopped
1 cup good quality red wine
4 cups beef stock
4 cups chicken stock
1 bay leaf

Preheat oven to 350°F. Season the short ribs evenly on all sides with the salt and pepper. Heat half of the oil over high heat in a large, oven-proof sauté pan or roasting pan. Add the ribs in a single layer and sear until nicely caramelized on each side, about 3–4 minutes. Remove from the heat once browned.

Meanwhile, heat the remaining oil in a large sauce pot over medium high to high heat and add the carrots, celery root, celery ribs, and onion. Cook, stirring every few minutes, until nicely caramelized, about 6–8 minutes. Add the red wine to the vegetables, deglazing, and stirring to pick up any brown bits. Reduce by two-thirds. Pour the mixture over the short ribs. Add the beef stock, chicken stock, and bay leaf, stirring the bottom of the roasting pan to pick up any browned bits. Bring the pan up to a simmer over high heat on the stovetop, cover with foil, place in the oven and cook until knife tender, about 2½ hours.

For the primary mash:

1 turnip, peeled and cut into a small dice

1 rutabaga, peeled and cut into a small dice

2 parsnips, peeled and cut into a small dice

2 carrots, peeled and cut into a small dice

1 large onion, peeled and cut into a small dice

2 tablespoons

1 tablespoon kosher salt or sea salt

1 teaspoon freshly ground black pepper

Toss all of the vegetables with the olive oil and salt and pepper. Place in a single layer on a roasting sheet or pan and cook in the same preheated oven until tender, about 30 minutes. When tender, place in a food mill or pulse in a food processor and puree until the mixture resembles a "relish."

For the potato mash:

4 large Yukon gold potatoes, peeled and cut into 1-inch cubes

Cold water to cover

1 tablespoon kosher or sea salt

1–1½ cups hot cream

3 tablespoons unsalted butter, room-temperature

Place the potatoes in a medium sauce pot. Cover the potatoes with cold water, add salt, bring up to a boil and reduce to a simmer over medium. Cook until the potatoes are knife tender, about 15 minutes. Drain well. Process through a food mill or with a manual masher, adding butter and streaming in the hot cream as you go. Taste and adjust seasoning as needed. To finish the mash, fold the warm roasted "primary" mash into the mashed potatoes. Reserve warm or re-heat over a water bath just before serving.

For the garnish:

2 cups fresh watercress

1 tablespoon best quality extra virgin olive oil

Sea or kosher salt and freshly ground pepper

To finish, remove the ribs from the braising liquid, reserving warm. Strain the liquid into a medium sauce pot, and discard the vegetable solids. Ladle off any excess fat and reduce cooking liquids to a sauce consistency, to nap a spoon. Adjust seasonings as needed. Plate one warm rib (or you can break them up a bit to spread to six portions) next to a generous mound of the warm mash. Spoon the warm sauce over each rib and garnish with a small mound of the dressed greens. (Note: the ribs, sauce, and mash can be prepared ahead, stored refrigerated and covered, for up to 2 days. Reheat ribs in a 350 oven, covered, until warm and the mash over a water bath.)

DONE TO YOUR LIKING STEAK DONENESS CHART

Although experts can gauge a steak's doneness level with a quick look and a clean poke, novices best use a meat thermometer, especially on expensive cuts of meat, to make sure it's prepared to your liking. Here's a chart to help you find your range:

Rare, 125°F to 130°F

Medium Rare, 130°F to 140°F

Medium, 140°F to 150°F

Medium Well, 150°F to 155°F

Well Done, 160°F

The Ocean Room

1 Sanctuary Beach Drive, Kiawah Island
(843) 768-6253
kiawahresort.com
Chef de Cuisine: Kyle Bowling

During the forty-five-minute drive from downtown to this breathtakingly beautiful barrier island, stress melts palpably away, like cold butter on a slow, easy simmer. The road weaves through arches of live oaks and marshes dappled with a dizzying dance of light swaying playfully with shade. By the time you're there, the vacation's begun, and The Ocean Room is the place to spend it.

The fanciest and priciest of the tony resort's restaurants, it is also the most beautiful, draped with swath upon swath of hand-wrought iron depicting marsh scenes and wildlife. The Mobil Four Star and AAA Four Diamond and Forbes 4 star restaurant recipient sits atop a sweeping staircase—think Scarlett and Rhett's posh Atlanta pad in *Gone with the Wind*.

Chef de Cuisine Kyle Bowling, has been working at the restaurant (although in different capacities) since it opened and hasn't changed anything "drastically" since. "I change seasonal items, of course, but our pursuit has always been continual refinement so everything evolves in some way. I grew up in a very rural area so I see a lot of parallels with traditional home-style foods making their way into restaurants. It's amazing how many different ways you can have shrimp and grits in Charleston. They have a hot brown where I'm from, that's kind of our shrimp and grits," Bowling explains.

"I constantly pursue refined gracious dining experiences for our guests by creating dishes that I would be excited to order, including a classic New York strip with a classic béarnaise sauce," says Bowling.

Here are some of Chef de Cuisine Bowling's rules for making the best steak possible:

"Buy beef from the local butcher shop. It costs a little more than the supermarket but the quality is much better, plus you have the bonus of talking to someone who knows how and where the meat is sourced. They also carry prime graded cuts that you can almost never find in regular grocery stores and you can usually find dry-aged cuts there, too, which is my personal favorite.

Always start with your grill (or broiler setting on your oven) at full heat. Toasting your pepper ahead of time will really enhance the flavor so begin by placing the peppercorns in a skillet over medium heat. Shake them constantly until they have a nutty, aromatic smell. Allow them to cool before grinding.

The real secret to cooking a great steak is resting it after it is cooked, for at least 5 minutes before you serve it. This will allow the heat to evenly distribute and keep the steak from bleeding out when it is cut."

GRILLED NEW YORK STRIP WITH BÉARNAISE SAUCE

(SERVES 4–6)

For the steak:

4–6 8-ounce New York Strip Steaks

2 tablespoons sea salt, finely ground

1 tablespoon black peppercorns, coarsely ground

2 tablespoons unsalted butter

For the Béarnaise Sauce:

3 cups clarified butter, prepared from 6 sticks unsalted butter (see directions below)

4 egg yolks

1 tablespoon white vinegar

1 teaspoon Piment d'Espelette (or substitute cayenne pepper)

Sea or kosher salt to taste

Leaves from 12 fresh tarragon branches, finely chopped

Before you get started, Chef Bowling recommends having your outside grill (or oven broiler) hot and ready to roll. Also have available a pair of tongs, 2 serving trays, a small skillet, pepper grinder, and a meat thermometer.

Lay out the steaks on a serving tray and sprinkle salt generously on all sides. Repeat with the pepper. Place steaks out on the grill with as much spacing between them as possible. Turn over steaks every 2–3 minutes until they are cooked to within 10°F of desired serving temperature (see Done to Your Liking sidebar, page 167).

Pull steaks off the grill and place them on the second, clean serving tray. Rub with butter and allow them to rest for at least 5 minutes before serving.

Heat clarified butter in a small saucepan over medium heat until it reaches 130°F. Separate the egg yolks into a large cup or medium plastic bowl. Add vinegar and Piment d'Espelette. Beat ("spin") the eggs briefly with the immersion blender. With the blender running, gradually drizzle in the warmed clarified butter until the eggs begin to emulsify with the butter. (It will start to thicken and look frothy). Continue adding butter at a steady rate at this point, being careful not to add enough butter to pool at the top. Add chopped tarragon and taste for seasoning. Store (up to 1 hour) in a warm area (a thermos works best).

Serve warm sauce over rested steaks and enjoy!

* The best way to clarify butter at home is to bring it to a boil and then cool it in the refrigerator. The butter will separate and become solid again and the water can be poured off. This can be prepared several days ahead, covered and refrigerated for several days.

Slightly North of Broad (S.N.O.B.)

192 East Bay Street, downtown
(843) 723-3424
snobcharleston.com
Chef Emeritus/Cuisine Commando: Frank Lee
Executive Chef: Russ Moore

No conversation about Charleston's cuisine scene would be complete without mention of Frank Lee and his myriad groundbreaking contributions. A true titan of taste and a South Carolina native, Frank is a self-taught cook who's been cooking professionally since the early '70s and who led the elite chefs' posse in Charleston's post–Hurricane Hugo culinary maturation.

A French classical technique devotee, Frank's dressed-down toque comes in the form of a red chile pepper baseball cap. You can barely follow his bobbing, busy head as he navigates the open kitchen here, where he's taught and groomed some of Charleston's finest chefs and servers.

S.N.O.B. was recently acquired by Hall Management Group (of Rita's Seaside Grill, Halls Chophouse, and Old Village Post House Inn's fame), and Frank also recently retired, but he still keeps his legendary cooking imprint on the menu in the capable hands of Executive Chef Russ Moore.

S.N.O.B.'s menu of contemporary Southern compositions with a strong vegetarian and ethnic leaning changes daily but maintains core favorites such as the Maverick Beef Tenderloin. "It's a take on veal Oscar. I turned it into beef with crab and béarnaise with a really good pepper sauce," says Frank. "The menu is really a composite of the people I've worked for and the people who have worked for me. We [with Moore] just find ways to make them [the recipes] more interesting," says the still humble, celebrated chef.

S.N.O.B. is a pretty, feminine restaurant, so named because it lies just a few blocks north of Broad Street, what locals think of as the dividing line between those with means (and local bloodlines) and those with less. For the record, those who live below Broad are known as S.O.B.s, yet another example of Charlestonians' wily wit.

Grilled Maverick Beef Tenderloin with Deviled Crab Cake, Béarnaise, and Green Peppercorn Sauce

(SERVES 6)

For the devil crab mix:

1 pound crab claws, picked

2 tablespoons yellow mustard

¼ cup whole cream

1¼ cups cracker meal (savory crackers such as Saltines, smashed and ground)

1 egg

6 dashes Tabasco sauce

1 tablespoon fresh-squeezed lemon juice

¼ cup green or red bell pepper, finely diced

¼ cup red onion, finely diced

½ teaspoon salt

½ teaspoon black pepper, freshly ground

1 quart vegetable oil

For the green peppercorn sauce:

1 tablespoon butter

1 small red onion, finely diced

1 teaspoon salt, plus more to taste

½ cup brandy

1 quart reduced veal stock (unsalted stock that's been reduced by half)

2 tablespoons green peppercorns, drained

For the béarnaise:

3 egg yolks

1 teaspoon salt

3 tablespoons water

½ cup fresh-squeezed lemon juice

2 dashes Tabasco sauce

½ bunch tarragon, stemmed and finely chopped, plus more for garnish (optional)

8 ounces (2 sticks) unsalted butter, at room temperature

For the tenderloin:

6 6- to 8-ounce beef tenderloins

Salt and freshly ground black pepper

Prepare the devil crab mix. Combine all the ingredients except 1 cup of the cracker meal and the vegetable oil in a medium bowl, mixing gently with a wooden spoon. Allow to rest at room temperature for 1 hour.

Meanwhile, prepare the green peppercorn sauce. Heat the butter, onion, and salt together over medium heat in a medium saucepan. Cook until the onion has softened, about 5 minutes. Add the brandy, increase the heat to medium-high, and reduce the brandy to a thick glaze. Add the reduced veal stock and bring to a simmer over medium-high heat. Reduce the sauce until it's thickened and shiny, skimming off any foam with a ladle. Add peppercorns and salt to taste. Set aside.

Next, prepare the béarnaise. Remember, this is an emulsion sauce, so temperature is important to prevent the sauce from breaking. Make this just before you grill the steak and cook the crab cakes, and keep it warm (at 145°F) for a few minutes at room temperature or for longer over a gentle water bath. To make the sauce, combine the egg yolks, salt, and water in a mixing bowl. Place over a pot of boiling water and whisk until the eggs begin to thicken and the sauce temperature reaches 145°F. Remove from the heat. Add lemon juice, Tabasco, and tarragon. Return the sauce to the water bath or heat and whisk until all ingredients are incorporated. Add the butter, 1 tablespoon at a time, whisking constantly, to create a thick and fluffy sauce. Set aside.

Form the crab cakes into 3-ounce patties and dust in the remaining 1 cup of cracker meal. Heat the oil to 350°F in a large pot over medium-high heat. Fry the cakes until they're golden brown all over, 3–5 minutes. Remove and drain on paper towels. Season lightly with salt.

Heat the grill to medium high. Season the tenderloin with salt and pepper. When the grill is hot cook meat to desired doneness and remove. Let it rest 5–10 minutes.

To assemble the dish, reheat the sauces if necessary. Dress each plate with a few spoonfuls of green peppercorn sauce. Place tenderloin in the center of each plate and top with a hot crab cake. Top this with a few spoonfuls of warm béarnaise. Dress each plate with a sprig of fresh tarragon if desired.

Lewis Barbecue

464 N. Nassau Street, upper peninsula
(843)805-9500
lewisbarbecue.com
Pitmaster: John Lewis

Custom-built smokers, a good rub, the best cuts, lots of love, and eighteen hours of a very low, slow burn over oak are the maxims of El Paso native John Lewis's Texas-style cue. "It's not necessarily Texas barbecue, but it's made in Texas. One of the hallmarks of that area is that you're making something that doesn't need sauce, because it's that delicious," says the Pitmaster.

Lewis began honing his craft at the tender age of 18 when his parents gave him a smoker. Eventually, he opened Le Barbecue in Austin in 2012, garnering multiple Pitmaster awards, and brought his smokers and talent to Charleston in 2016. They come in droves for his prime brisket (Lewis calls it the highest quality and so well marbled it practically bastes itself), beef short ribs, beef back ribs, and more, all cut to order and served on butcher paper. Lewis serves sauce on the side, if desired. "Typically the Texas barbecue sauce is a red, ketchup-based sauce with a lot of black pepper and some chiles," says Lewis.

Sauce or no, it's not barbecue without the sides. Because Lewis wasn't willing to share his smoking, rub, or sauce recipes, we decided to use this sweet, creamy, crusty on the bottom corn pudding as the brisket pairing ticket. Lewis grew up in El Paso near his great grandparent's chile farm in Hatch, New Mexico, where the chile in the pudding is grown. "It's similar to an Anaheim, but it's a bit spicier with a grassy flavor. It picks up the flavors of the terroir in Hatch," says Lewis. If you can't find one, substitute Anaheim peppers, or use canned Hatch peppers already roasted and peeled. Lewis prefers a top quality, high-end cast iron pan, because the iron is denser and less porous so stuff doesn't stick to it too much. Get the cast iron hot in the oven first, before putting in the pudding mixture. It will ensure a super crispy bottom, "almost like a Detroit style pizza," says Lewis.

HATCH GREEN CHILE CORN PUDDING

(SERVES 4–6)

2–3 Hatch green chiles
1½ cups frozen corn kernels
¼ cup all-purpose flour
¼ cup yellow cornmeal
2 tablespoons granulated sugar
1 teaspoon kosher salt
½ teaspoon baking powder
¼ teaspoon granulated garlic
3 large eggs
⅔ cup heavy cream
½ cup mild cheddar cheese, cut into ½-inch cubes
¾ cup fresh corn kernels (cut from one ear of fresh corn)
2 tablespoons unsalted butter
¼ cup shredded mild cheddar cheese

Roast the Hatch green chiles over a hot, open flame until the skins blacken and separate (about 4-5 minutes each side). Place the roasted chiles in a plastic bag and allow them to steam (in their own heat) for 1 hour. Peel the skins and remove the seeds, discarding both the seeds and charred skins. In a food processor, roughly chop the chiles. This should yield about ¼ cup roasted chiles. Defrost the frozen corn kernels and chop in a food processor until pureed.

Combine the flour, yellow cornmeal, granulated sugar, salt, baking powder, and granulated garlic in a mixing bowl and blend together until homogeneous. In a separate mixing bowl, beat the eggs and whisk in the heavy cream. Add the frozen corn puree, chopped and roasted Hatch green chiles, cubed mild cheddar cheese, and fresh corn kernels. Pour the dry ingredients in the wet ingredients. Whisk together until homogeneous.

Preheat the oven to 375°F with a medium cast iron pan. When hot, take the heated cast iron pan out of the oven and add the butter. Allow butter to heat until foaming and milk solids are lightly toasted. Be sure to allow the butter to fully coat the bottom. Pour the corn pudding batter into the hot cast iron pan with foaming butter. Sprinkle the shredded mild cheddar cheese on the batter and return to the oven. Cook for 30 minutes at 375°F. The cheese should be nicely browned and the pudding should be set, but not firm in the center. Allow to rest for 5 minutes and serve warm

SASSY SOUTHERN BARBECUE SAUCES

Like Texan's, South Carolinians take a lot of pride in their 'cue which is often long, slow roasted pig cooked whole and later chopped or "pulled" and doused with a puckery sauce. In North and South Carolina, you'll run across one of three types: a vinegar/hot pepper flake sauce, a mustard sauce and variations on a tomato-based sauce.

RODNEY SCOTT'S WHOLE HOG BBQ

1011 King Street, upper peninsula
(843) 990-9535
rodneyscottsbbq.com
Owner/Pitmaster: Rodney Scott

Rodney Scott literally grew up smoking pigs and perfecting barbecue. "I was an only child. I was there and they had to take me everywhere they went," he affably remarks. "There" for Rodney's parents was Scott's Variety Store in Hemingway, South Carolina, about 110 miles from Charleston in the heart of the Pee Dee, South Carolina 'cue country. Behind the store were massive pits designed for housing butterflied, whole hogs for 12-hour slow smokes over oak, hickory, and pecan wood. The pigs were mopped at the end with an elixir of vinegar, pepper, a few lemons, and as Rodney says, "a whole lotta love."

Sadly, a massive fire temporarily took out the store in 2014. Though no one was hurt, it was a devastating loss for the family business. Rodney, with the help and support of some of his Charleston chef buddies, went on an "Exile Tour," which had the Pitmaster on the road for eighteen days cooking barbecue throughout the Southeast. The tour raised enough money for him to rehabilitate the property in Hemingway, give some back to help others in similar situations, and to open his Charleston Whole Hog BBQ in late 2017.

Rodney basically does the same thing at the new, 66-seat location that he's always done. "I'm the same old country boy I always was. You have to love this work to do it all day. It's one of the toughest [physically] things to do. But I do love it." His signature sauce (the exact recipe will not be shared!) is more of an Eastern North Carolina sauce with its vinegar and heat intensity, than a South Carolina Sauce.

Collards are a classic barbecue side dish, but not all are made the same. "I was never a collards fan, but I know the aroma and look of it. I added some stuff, like my sauce, to kind of go against the grain and add something special that makes you feel like you got a slap upside the head wondering exactly what's in there." His special sauce is available at the restaurant, so consider making a trip to Charleston to get some for these stellar greens that makes enough for 4–6, depending on how "greedy" those persons are, says Scott.

ONE WAY
RS

RODNEY SCOTT'S BBQ COLLARD GREENS

(SERVES 4–6)

½ cup rendered pork fat (or substitute pork stock)

1 medium yellow onion (about 1 cup), medium dice

2 teaspoons garlic cloves, minced

2 pounds (about 6–7 cups) fresh collard greens, stemmed, thoroughly washed, and cut into 1-inch squares,

1 quart (4 cups) water

¾ pound pork skin (or substitute a smoked ham hock)

1 tablespoon + 1 teaspoon kosher salt

1 tablespoon Rodney's BBQ Sauce (or substitute another vinegar-based BBQ Sauce)

2 tablespoons apple cider vinegar

In a large heavy bottom pot over medium heat, add the rendered pork. Add the diced onion and garlic and sauté until they become translucent, about 5–7 minutes. Add the greens, water, and pork skin to the pot. Cover and simmer until greens are completely tender, about 45 minutes. Season the greens with salt, sauce, and vinegar. Reserve warm before serving.

HALLS CHOPHOUSE

434 King Street, downtown
(843) 727-0090
hallschophouse.com
Corporate Executive Chef Hall Management Group: Matthew Niessner

As much as it is about steaks (Allen Brothers of Chicago dry-aged and wet-aged steaks, that is), Halls is 100 percent about personalized care of their clients. From the Hall family members that are almost always there to greet and chat with clientele, to the bartenders and servers that know regulars by name, one feels deliciously tended to here.

Nobody understands that better than well-seasoned restaurant veteran and Corporate Executive Chef Hall Management group than Matthew Niessner. "I need to understand our clients in order to execute my job well," says the chef who, when presented the opportunity, likes to craft a personalized menu for diners. But not just a dish, he likes to weave an entire experience starting with the right cocktail, the appetizer, the entrée and several select sides and desserts. "My philosophy and passion lies in the experience of the diner. We really want to deliver an entire experience."

Halls feels very masculine with dark paneled walls and inviting banquettes. It recalls a classic steak house of a bygone era. "It feels like it's been here forever, so old that if we could have cigars in the bar and martinis at lunch, we would," jokes Niessner. But, old school is the intent and at Halls steaks reign supreme. "We do great steaks; the consistency, the char, the blister. Also, the family-style sides we offer and salads and appetizers."

So, as he likes to do for his guests, Niessner requested to share his ideas on how to make the best steak (compare to The Ocean Room's Chef Bowling's tips, page 168) and what best to pair it with in a selection of Halls most interesting side dishes. As he says, "Anyone can do creamed spinach!" To follow is what Chef Niessner recommends for a "wonderful, steak cookout event at home." He suggests pairing the meal with a nice Petite Sirah or big Cabernet Sauvignon.

Here's the general plan of attack as outlined by Niessner: Prepare the cream corn in advance and have it in a baking dish. Prepare all the salad ingredients and display on a platter, reserving the dressing until dinner time. While the steaks are on the grill, the corn should be baking in the oven at 350°F for 8 minutes. Place the steaks on individual dinner plates, set the corn in the center of the table with the salad, and dress the salad.

CREAMED CORN

(SERVES 8)

12 ears of corn, roasted with husks on

¾ pounds (1½ sticks) unsalted butter

1 red bell pepper, seeded and finely diced

1 Vidalia onion, finely diced

2 cloves garlic, slivered

2½ teaspoons Crystal hot sauce

2¼ cups rice flour (may substitute all-purpose flour if not making gluten free)

2 tablespoons grated nutmeg

½ gallon (8 cups) whole milk

1 quart (4 cups) half and half

3 cups yellow cheddar cheese, grated

2¾ cups pepper jack cheese, grated

Kosher or sea salt and freshly ground black pepper to taste

Preheat oven to 375°F. Place the corn on bare oven rack with husk on for 30 minutes, or until husk browns. Let cool and cut corn from the cob.

Meanwhile prepare the Mornay Sauce base. Melt the butter in a medium saucepot over medium heat. Add the bell pepper, Vidalia, garlic, and hot sauce. Cook gently, stirring, until the vegetables have softened, about 5 minutes. Add the flour all at once and stir to combine. Cook for one minute to cook out flour taste. Add the nutmeg, milk, and half and half, whisking to incorporate. Increase heat to medium high. Continue cooking, whisking until the sauce thickens and comes to a low boil, 5–7 minutes. Add the cheddar and pepper jack cheeses. Whisk to incorporate. Add the corn and heat through. If too thick, add more half and half. If too loose, add more pepper jack cheese. Taste and adjust seasoning as needed.

ICEBERG WEDGE SALAD WITH BLUE CHEESE DRESSING

(SERVES 8)

For the bleu cheese dressing:

1 pint mayonnaise

1½ teaspoons shallots, finely chopped

1 teaspoon garlic, finely minced

¼ cup Italian parsley, finely chopped

½ cups sour cream

4 tablespoons fresh lemon juice

1 tablespoon white wine vinegar

¾ cup crumbled buttermilk bleu cheese

Sea or kosher salt and freshly ground black pepper to taste

¼ teaspoon cayenne pepper

For the salad:

16 pieces of thick-cut sliced bacon (preferably Neuskes brand)

2 heads iceberg lettuce

2 yellow tomatoes

2 red tomatoes

4 avocados

1 bunch of green onions, base and tips removed, coarsely chopped

2 tablespoons extra virgin olive oil

To prepare the blue cheese dressing, simply stir together all of the ingredients in a medium bowl using a wooden spoon until combined. Cover and chill for at least 1 hour. (Note: The dressing can be prepared and refrigerated two days ahead.)

For the salad, preheat oven to 350°F. Lay the bacon across two baking sheets, in a single layer. Bake the bacon for 8 minutes, or until crispy. Core the iceberg and cut into quarters. Cut each tomato in half and slice each half in two. Split and peel avocado and slice each half (one half avocado per serving).

To serve, arrange the iceberg on a platter, putting the bacon in the center of the iceberg. Arrange the sliced tomatoes around the outside of the iceberg. Drizzle the iceberg lettuce with the blue cheese dressing. Arrange the avocado on top of the iceberg and drizzle with green onions and olive oil.

RIBEYE

(SERVES 8)

8 16-ounce prime or ribeye steaks from your local butcher

8 tablespoons of kosher salt

2 tablespoons of coarse ground black pepper

3 tablespoons canola oil

Mix the pepper and salt mixture together. On a baking pan pour half the oil and sprinkle half the salt and pepper mixture evenly. Introduce the steaks to the pan. Pour the remainder of the oil over the steaks and season with the remaining salt and pepper mixture. Press to evenly distribute the oil and seasoning. Let the tray of ribeyes stand at room temperature for 10 minutes while the grill is heating up.

Add the steaks to a hot grill. Be careful not to flame up too much. Cook on each side for about 4 minutes, depending on desired internal temperature (see steak doneness chart, page 167). Assemble the rest of the items while the steaks are resting for 5 minutes.

Poultry Perch

Birds of all feathers have long flocked together in Lowcountry kitchens. Chicken, an affordable and broadly interpreted ingredient in the South and in Charleston, is perhaps most beloved in its slyly simple form—fried. James Beard Award winner Robert Stehling treats his buttermilk-soaked birds to a bath of spiced peach gravy at Hominy Grill. Meanwhile, chicken heads south of the border with Santiago Zavalza's sunny take on Pollo Mole Verde at Santi's. Two types of chicken taco preparations, one from Basico and another Mex 1 Coastal Cantina, both take their deep flavor cues from zesty, tenderizing brines and crackle with tortilla freshness and crunchy condiments. Rutledge Cab Co.'s pillowy hand-made gnocchi gives an especially smooth and soul-warming edge to Executive Chef Jeff Marshburn's chicken and dumplings.

When autumn's chill eases into Charleston's usually balmy air, around late October, camouflage clothing and gun gear emerge like so many birds heading south for winter. Duck, geese, quail, and other fowl start showing up on restaurant menus in inventive preparations. Cannon Green's Amalia Scatena's Roasted Quail with Chicken Liver Gravy and Fontina Polenta is a favorite at the restaurant and her family's Christmas table feast. Jeremiah Bacon's back in this chapter with The Macintosh's "rustic elegant" take on stuffed quail with farro and root vegetables.

HOMINY GRILL

207 Rutledge Avenue, downtown
(843) 937-0930
hominygrill.com
Chef/Owner: Robert Stehling

Robert Stehling is a perfect amalgamation of his cooking-intensive childhood in Greensboro, North Carolina, his professional experience, and his artistic, beat-of-his-own-drummer personality. As a kid, he canned and preserved produce from his family's huge organic garden, getting close to food and his Southern roots. Later, the University of North Carolina art major needed a job and picked up an apron and sponge to wash dishes at the celebrated Crook's Corner in Chapel Hill. "It was unbelievable there. All the dishwashers had PhDs. It was almost like a commune. There was a fabulous focus on Southern food there," says Robert. Six years later, he "turned loose" and made a working tour of some of Manhattan's best restaurants before coming down to Charleston to open Hominy Grill.

Mostly known for its hearty, Southern breakfasts and sturdy working lunches, Hominy also puts out stunning dinners in its quiet single-house setting on the medical side of town. After years of accolades, Robert achieved one of the highest kinds of praise, receiving the James Beard Best Southeastern Chef award in 2008, something that he sincerely says "surprised" him a little. Considering that this man can make something as simple as squash casserole or mac 'n' cheese taste like fresh descents from heaven and biscuits so high and light they practically touch it, this happy news should have come as no surprise at all. This is some of the best food you can eat in Charleston or in the South. Don't even get me started on the chocolate pudding or buttermilk pie. In the recipe that follows, Robert sticks with Del Monte spiced canned peaches for "something extra." They can be found in most grocery stores in the South.

FRIED CHICKEN WITH SPICED PEACH GRAVY

(SERVES 5–6)

For the fried chicken:

1 3- to 3½-pound chicken

1 cup buttermilk

2 cups peanut oil

1 cup all-purpose flour

2 teaspoons salt

2 teaspoons freshly ground black pepper

For the spiced peach gravy:

2 tablespoons butter

¼ cup onion, minced

2 tablespoons all-purpose flour

Salt and freshly ground black pepper, to taste

1 cup chicken stock

½ cup Del Monte spiced peaches, chopped

¼–½ cup syrup from the canned peaches

Cut the chicken into eight evenly sized pieces, leaving the bones in and the skin intact. Place the chicken and the buttermilk in a large bowl, toss to coat, and marinate for at least 2 hours. Heat the oil over medium-high heat in a large cast-iron skillet. Combine the flour and the salt and pepper in a paper bag and drop the chicken into the bag, tossing to coat evenly. Shake off any excess flour and begin to fry the chicken, starting with the dark pieces, then following with the white pieces. Reduce the heat to medium, cover the skillet, and fry 15 minutes. Remove the cover, turn each piece of chicken over, and fry, uncovered, for another 10–15 minutes. Remove the chicken carefully with tongs and drain on paper towels.

Meanwhile, make the gravy. Drain and discard all but 1 tablespoon of the oil used for frying. Heat the skillet over medium heat and add the butter and onion. Cook, stirring, until the onion is golden, about 5 minutes. Lightly season the flour with salt and pepper, then whisk it into the gravy and cook, stirring, until golden brown. Whisk in the chicken stock, bring to a boil over high heat, and whisk until thickened slightly. Add the peaches and the syrup to the skillet and reduce the heat to low. Simmer for 4–5 minutes. Season to taste with salt and pepper.

To serve, put a piece or two of chicken on each plate and top with a generous amount of peach gravy. The chicken is excellent with home-style mashed potatoes.

Cypress

167 East Bay Street, downtown
(843) 727-0111
magnolias-blossom-cypress.com
Executive Chef: Craig Deihl

Craig Deihl was just 23-years-old in 2001 when he assumed the head role at Cypress. He admits with his signature candor that his culinary personality was still evolving at the time. Indeed, then more retro and clubbish, dishing out classics like chateaubriand and tableside Caesar salads, these days Cypress and Craig are all grown up, serving new-world, classically-interpreted Lowcountry creations in the restaurant's Old-World, nineteenth-century warehouse setting.

The restaurant's stunning and dramatic interior—which houses a wall of wine and features a bird's-eye view of the spacious kitchen from a sophisticated upstairs bar—is the perfect backdrop to Craig's goodies, from house-made, grass-fed beef and local pork pepperonis and hams to the local, seasonal produce he weaves into his edible bag of tricks. Craig likes to build dishes that utilize the entire palate—hot, salty, bitter—to create memorable taste parades, as in the recipe that follows. "Colorful and piquant, this chicken recipe is a nice way to show off with exotic blood oranges. They have a deeper flavor than traditional oranges and are commonly available in produce sections during the fall and early winter season," says Craig.

Although Cypress recently closed, this entry was kept in the book due to its longstanding relevance and love on the Charleston food scene and Chef Deihl's talent.

PAN-ROASTED CHICKEN WITH BABY BEETS, ARTICHOKES, AND BLOOD ORANGE VINAIGRETTE

(SERVES 4)

For the vinaigrette:

¼ cup fresh-squeezed blood orange juice

¼ cup sherry vinegar

1 tablespoon shallot, minced

2 tablespoons honey

4 tablespoons extra-virgin olive oil

1½ teaspoons salt

Pinch of white pepper

1 tablespoon chives, minced

For the artichokes:

¼ cup fresh-squeezed lemon juice

4 cups water

10 cocktail artichokes (about 1 pound)

Fresh basil, thyme, and tarragon sprigs (3 each)

¼ cup white wine

2 tablespoons salt

½ teaspoon white pepper

For the beets:

6 baby (golf ball–sized) beets

2 tablespoons olive oil

2 tablespoons white wine vinegar

2 teaspoons salt

Pinch of white pepper

For the chicken:

4 boneless chicken breasts

Salt and white pepper to taste

¼ cup canola oil, or as needed

3 tablespoons butter

1 tablespoon thyme leaves, finely chopped

4 chive tips, for garnish

Begin with the vinaigrette. In a small mixing bowl, combine all of the ingredients except the minced chives, and whisk. Refrigerate, covered, until ready to use. (The vinaigrette can be prepared a day ahead.)

Next, prepare the artichokes. In a medium saucepan, combine the lemon juice and water. Peel away the outer leaves of the artichokes. Place the artichokes on a cutting board and cut the top of the artichoke, where the leaves start to change from yellow to green, about ½ inch from the top. Peel the stems and trim away the firm green skin with a paring knife. Place the artichokes in the lemon water. Wrap a couple sprigs of each herb with kitchen string, creating a little herb bundle (bouquet garni). Add the bouquet garni, the white wine, and salt and pepper to the saucepan. Place pan over medium heat and bring to a simmer. Cook for 35 minutes or until the artichokes are fork-tender. Remove from heat and allow the artichokes to cool in the liquid. Remove the bouquet garni and discard. Slice the artichokes in half vertically and return to the liquid. Set aside.

To prepare the beets, preheat the oven to 350°F. Place the beets on a large sheet of aluminum foil and mix with the remaining ingredients, tossing to coat. Wrap the foil around the beets to form a tight package, making sure there are no openings in the foil pack. Place on a sheet pan and roast for about 45 minutes, depending on the actual size of the beets. They are done when they are fork-tender. Remove from the oven, carefully open the foil pack to release steam, and allow the beets to cool. Drain any juice and reserve for when the beets are reheated. Use a rubbing motion with a clean kitchen towel to pry the skin loose from the beets. (Chef Craig recommends wearing gloves to prevent the juice from turning fingers pink.) Slice the stem off each beet and cut into quarters.

To prepare the chicken, season the chicken breasts on both sides with salt and pepper. Place a large sauté pan over medium heat and add the oil to a depth of ⅛ inch. Heat until the oil is hot and starting to move around in the pan. Carefully lay the chicken breasts skin side down in the pan. Cook for 4 minutes, reduce heat to medium-low, and cook for 5 more minutes. Turn the chicken and cook for 6 minutes on the second side. Add the butter and thyme to the pan and baste the chicken with the juices, using a spoon, for a full 2 minutes. The chicken should be done at this point: the juices will run clear and it will have an internal temperature of 160°F. Remove from the pan and place the chicken on clean kitchen towels. Allow to rest for 5 minutes.

To finish the dish, whisk the remaining chives into room-temperature vinaigrette. Reheat the beets over low heat in a saucepan with their reserved juices and gently reheat the artichokes in their cooking juice for 5 minutes, over medium-low heat. Slice the chicken into 1-inch-thick slices on the bias just before serving. To plate, place a combination of beets and artichokes alongside a pool of the vinaigrette. Top with the sliced chicken breast and garnish each with a chive tip.

Santi's Restaurante Mexicano

1302 Meeting Street Road, uptown Charleston, (843) 722-2633
1471 Ben Sawyer Boulevard, Mount Pleasant, (843)288-3146
santisrestaurantemexicano.com
Owners: Jeff Hefel and Santiago Zavalza

No matter how hard you try, it is virtually impossible not to reorder the same thing you had the first time you entered Santi's flawlessly flavorful realm. It's like the first love you'll never forget and to whom no one else can compare. For me, it's the mole and verde sauces, but everybody has their own Santi's love story.

Something of a sleeper when the original location opened on a lonely end of Meeting Street Road in 2004, Santi's quickly became a local favorite for exceptional and authentic Mexican food prepared by Mexico native Santiago Zavalza. "You need to know the flavors and how things are supposed to cook to do it right. And, no shortcuts!" he explains. Whole fresh chickens are poached in huge pots with a head of garlic and a whole onion for Santi's flavorful chicken, which is served with a mole verde sauce that pops with peppery pungency.

Former agricultural engineer and substitute teacher Jeff Hefel applies his mathematical mind to balancing the books and his natural affability at the front of the small house, overseeing the lively crowd of bankers, bikers, and other assorted types who regularly flock to the restaurant.

At Santi's, the chicken is paired with Spanish rice, black beans, fat avocado slices, and corn tortillas. The chicken is also excellent wrapped up in a soft tortilla, topped with the sauce and cheese, and heated in the oven for a winning enchilada.

Pollo Mole Verde (Chicken in Green Sauce)

(SERVES 4–6)

6 chicken leg quarters, skin on
5 garlic cloves
½ yellow onion
3 16-ounce cans tomatillos, well drained
6 whole jalapeños
3 chicken bouillon cubes
Freshly ground black pepper to taste
3 tablespoons vegetable oil
Salt to taste

Place the chicken in a large pot and add water to cover. Add 3 of the garlic cloves and the onion and bring to a boil over high heat. Then reduce to a simmer and cook until the chicken is tender and cooked through, about 40 minutes. When the chicken is done, drain it well and set aside. When cool enough to handle, pull the chicken from the bones in long, thick shreds. Discard the bones and skin.

To make the sauce, combine the tomatillos, jalapeños, 2 garlic cloves, bouillon cubes, and a pinch of black pepper in the bowl of a food processor or blender. Blend until chunky-smooth, about 2 minutes. Set aside.

Heat the oil in a large, deep pan over medium-high heat. When hot, add the sauce and the chicken. Reduce the heat to low and simmer gently for about 10 minutes or until hot throughout. Season to taste with salt and pepper. Serve hot with Santi's favorite garnishes, as suggested above, or use some of your own favorites.

Basico

4399 McCarthy Street
(843) 471-1670
basicombrc.com
Executive Chef: Adam R. Miller

At first glance, the cheerful stripes, refreshing aquamarine colors, massive shimmering swimming pool, communal greens and gardens, and the shiny spot that is Basico, you may think you've stumbled upon a posh country club with a private restaurant. The set-up (on the edge of popular Park Circle), while appealing, can be a tad confusing to the uninitiated. In fact, Basico is a public restaurant situated under the figurative and literal umbrella of a private membership club called Mixson Bath & Raquet Club.

But there is nothing confusing about the food, which is offered both to private members and the general public at the restaurant. Executive Chef Adam R. Miller makes sure of that. The Art Institute of Charleston culinary grad's mother knew his destiny well before he did. "She told me to go to culinary school when I was a kid," he laughs. But seriously, he worked his way through the front and back of several restaurant houses (including Amen Street, page 73) honing his craft, his skills and personal style, which he describes as more "Southern classic, meat and two sides and no tweezers." While he's apt to apply the Southern casual side more for the club menu, he digs deep into fine dining technique with a farm-to-table mood and presentation at Basico.

For extra Mexican authenticity, Miller refers to a couple of excellent Mexican cookbooks and the wisdom of his Mexican prep "girls" staff. "They're all natives of Oaxaca, Mexico, which is the Mecca of Mexican moles. They're about thirty moles that come from Oaxaca. We have three moles on the menu and not one even resembles a chocolate sauce, which is how many Americans think of them," says Miller.

His buttermilk fried chicken takes a long brine soak and then is dipped in buttermilk before being breaded and fried, the way the best fried chicken should, as any Tennessee-born chef like Miller knows. The delectable taco is adorned with a crunchy, creamy, zesty array of condiments that are as beautiful to look at as they are to eat. At Basico, the corn tortillas are made fresh every morning. Find the best quality you can. Also, Adluh chicken breader used for breading the chicken is a blended and seasoned breading mix that is available online and in specialty shops.

Buttermilk Fried Chicken with Pickled Jicama, Spicy Aioli, Queso Fresco, and Cilantro

(SERVES 8)

For the chicken brine:

2 quarts (8 cups) water

1 cup kosher or sea salt

½ teaspoon cumin seed

1 teaspoon fennel seed

1 star anise

1 bay leaf

½ teaspoon red pepper flakes

½ teaspoon dill seed

1 tablespoon yellow mustard seed

½ cinnamon stick

1 teaspoon coriander seed

1 teaspoon brown sugar

1 tablespoon black peppercorns

2 allspice berries (or dash ground allspice)

2 fresh thyme sprigs

¼ cup molasses

2 lemon rind strips

16 chicken tenders

For the Pickled Jicama:

1 cup white wine or apple cider vinegar

1 cup water

⅓ cup granulated sugar

1 root ball (about 1 pound) jicama, peeled and cut into ¼" x ¼" x 2" thick matchsticks

For the Spicy Aioli:

2 cups Duke's Mayonnaise (See Sidebar on Duke's, page 18)

¼ cup Valentina hot sauce (or substitute another brand)

½ teaspoon fresh lemon juice

¼ cup fresh cilantro, finely chopped

For the chicken and tacos:

16 chicken tenders, brined and drained

2 cups buttermilk

2 cups Adluh Chicken Breader (or other seasoned breading mix)

6 cups peanut or vegetable oil for frying, as needed

1 cup queso fresco Mexican cheese, crumbled

8 corn tortillas

16 fresh cilantro leaves, for garnish

The day before, prepare the brine and brine the chicken. Combine all of the brine ingredients and bring to a boil in a large pot. Remove from heat and refrigerate until completely cool. Place chicken tenders in the cooled liquid and brine overnight, at least 12 hours. Remove chicken from the brine and dry thoroughly, patting dry with paper towels.

To prepare the pickled jicama, place vinegar, water, and sugar in a medium pot and bring to a boil over high heat. Place the jicama matchsticks in a medium bowl. When the pickle mixture comes to a boil, remove from the heat and pour it over the cut jicama, using just enough to cover the jicama. Allow to cool at room temperature for 15 minutes and then place into refrigerator, covered, to cool completely. Once cool it is ready for use. (Note: Best if done a day ahead just to ensure they are cooled and properly pickled.)

A few hours before frying the chicken and compiling the tacos, prepare the aioli by simply mixing the ingredients together in a small bowl. Cover and refrigerate.

If a deep fryer is available, this is the easiest way to fry the chicken. If not, Chef Adam suggests a cast iron skillet, with enough oil to fry the chicken which should be covered by at least 1-inch of oil heated to 325°F. Pour the buttermilk into a medium bowl and carefully place the chicken tenders in the buttermilk. One by one, take the chicken from the buttermilk and coat in the Adluh chicken breader, being sure to evenly coat the chicken. Place the breaded chicken into your fryer or frying pan, being careful not to overcrowd the fryer or the chicken will be soggy instead of crispy. Cook the chicken to an internal temperature of 165°F. Use the oven to keep already cooked pieces warm at the lowest oven setting while the rest cook.

Assemble the tacos. Warm the tortillas briefly in the oven. Place two pieces of chicken on top of each tortilla. Drizzle some spicy aioli on top. Top this with a few pieces of the pickled jicama. Sprinkle a generous dose of queso fresco and finish with a few leaves of fresh cilantro. Serve hot.

Mex 1 Coastal Cantina

817 St. Andrews Boulevard, West Ashley, (843) 751-4001
2205 Middle Street, Sullivan's Island, (843)882-8172
mex1coastalcantina.com
Culinary Director Mex 1 Group: Ryan Jones

A day of surf and sun is guaranteed to build an appetite for a cool après beach hang-out with light and refreshing food, washed down with some tequila or a cool brew. That's the name of the game at Mex 1 Coastal Cantina. It's named after Mexico 1, the interstate that runs parallel to the Baja, California peninsula, an area known for sweet surf, cantinas, and taco shops. And, it's owned by authentic surfers, people that care as much about surfers and the community as the food. "Every surfboard (and there are many) in this place has some connection to the surfing community," says Culinary Director Ryan Jones.

Jones, a New England native, came down to Charleston with his family after closing his restaurant near Hartford, Connecticut. Seeking a food-driven town, near the water in the South, he found it and fell in love at first sight with Charleston. The drift towards the team at Mex 1 group was natural, impromptu and casual and felt very right, according to Jones.

His job, when he started in early 2017, was to morph and streamline the menu into something more than tacos and tequilas, because it IS a coastal cantina. "You'll notice there are no heavy refried beans on the menu. We keep the core menu of tacos and Baja bowls, but my primary focus is the cantina side, moving even more towards a focus on seasonal items. For example, last week some gorgeous tuna poke came in, so we turned that into a poke bowl. Then, soft shell crabs were coming in and we did a fried soft shell, cabbage, carrot remoulade taco. We got our hands on some pork belly and made a slow-cooked pork belly and pimento cheese taco," Jones recalls. All were so popular customers were demanding them as regular menu items, and Jones imagines that some of these creations will become part of the super tasty menu. So tasty, a new location is scheduled to open in North Mount Pleasant by 2018.

Chef Ryan says this taco recipe is "all about the chicken." He starts by making a flavor-infused brine and

brining the chicken overnight. After 18 hours in the brine, the chicken is drained and dried for the next layer of flavor, "the smoke." The chicken is smoked for 2½ hours. This is the real base of flavor for the taco.

CANTINA CHICKEN TACO

(MAKES 16 TACOS)

For the chicken brine:

1 gallon water

1½ cups kosher salt

1 cup light brown sugar

1 fresh lemon, cut in half

1 fresh lime, cut in half

5 bay leaves

15 whole black peppercorns

1 teaspoon red pepper flakes

3 whole chickens, cut into 6 bone-in chicken breasts, and 6 legs, discarding the rest

4 cups ice

For the corn and black bean salsa:

1 cup Roma tomatoes, finely diced

1 cup red onion, finely diced

1 cups corn, cooked and cut off cob

1 cup canned black beans, drained

1 cup fresh cilantro, finely chopped
¼ cup jalapenos, seeded and finely chopped
1–2 tablespoons kosher salt
1½ teaspoons fresh lime juice
1½ teaspoons fresh garlic, minced
½ teaspoon ground black pepper

For the tacos:

16 flour tortillas, grilled
½ cup shredded red cabbage
1½ cups shredded green cabbage
16 lime wedges (4 limes, cut)
¾ cup cilantro, freshly chopped

Make the brine. In large pot combine water, kosher salt, brown sugar, lemons, limes, bay leaves, peppercorns, and red pepper flakes. Bring brine mixture to a boil. While brine is cooking place the chickens into a very large bowl, leaving enough room for brine. Once the brine boils, reduce to a simmer and cook for another 15 minutes. Remove brine from the pot and place in a large mixing bowl and rest the brine for 30 minutes. Then add ice and pour brine over chicken pieces. Cover and store the chicken in the refrigerator for 12–18 hours.

To smoke the chickens, arrange in a 250°F smoker with hickory for 2–2½ hours or until internal temperature is 165°F.

Meanwhile, prepare the corn and black bean salsa. Place the tomatoes, red onions, corn, black beans, cilantro, and jalapenos in a large bowl and hand mix to evenly combine. Add kosher salt, lime juice, garlic, and black pepper and gently hand mix to combine. Cover, refrigerated, until ready to use. (Note: the salsa will store well, refrigerated for 1 day.)

Now it's time to build the tacos. Toss to combine the red and green cabbage together in a medium bowl. Pull chicken meat off the bone removing the skin, but not over shredding. Keep it in chunky, long threads. Evenly distribute chicken in the center of each tortilla. Top the chicken with 1 tablespoon of corn and black bean salsa, and 1 tablespoon of blended shredded cabbage. Garnish taco with a lime wedge and freshly chopped cilantro.

Cannon Green

103 Spring Street, downtown
(843) 817-7311
cannongreencharleston.com

Culinary Director Easton Porter Group/Executive Chef: Amalia Scatena

Lime green French doors open into an invitingly verdant space peppered with generously padded green cushions on the bistro chairs that surround marble tables at this "gathering common" known as Cannon Green.

Appropriately, the kitchen at this utterly green restaurant is commanded by Executive Chef Amalia Scatena, who grew up in California where she was raised on extra virgin olive oil, fresh greens, herbs, edible flowers, and everything that was seasonal and fresh. "My parents were very food-forward. We grew up eating at restaurants that I know about now, because they're so well known (think Alice Waters and Chez Panisse). My brother's a chef, too. I always knew I wanted to do something with food (not necessarily a chef), my whole life," exclaims Scatena.

The Culinary Institute of Florence (Apicius) grad was stationed in the rolling hills of Virginia at elegant Pippin Hill Farm & Vineyards when Easton Porter Group (which also owns Zero George, see page 146) began forming Cannon Green's concept. Scatena came down to Charleston, was hooked, and ended up opening the restaurant and creating its menu which she describes as one where ingredients are "super important." Mediterranean shows up here and there and so does a lot of Charleston-grown-and-raised products.

Scatena has a personal fondness for quail, which goes back to her family. "My grandparents lived outside San Francisco, where they used to set a wire bird trap in the yard. Week after week a few quail would wander in, looking for food. By the end of December word had spread amongst the quail about the food in our yard and there would be fifty birds in there. On Christmas day, my grandparents would pull the little string that was attached to the kitchen window, trapping the birds and securing our Christmas feast. Many years and miles away from California and that quail trap, this meal has been our family Christmas tradition ever since," she enthusiastically explains.

Scatena purchases her quail from Manchester Farms Quail. You can order directly from them and request the semi-boneless for this recipe. It will make your work considerably lighter, the quail tastes exquisite, and the few bones that are left in the quail will help it to maintain its shape as it cooks.

ROASTED MANCHESTER FARMS QUAIL WITH CHICKEN LIVER GRAVY AND FONTINA POLENTA

(SERVES 4)

For the quail and gravy:

8 whole semiboneless quail

Coarse kosher salt and freshly cracked black pepper

3 tablespoons canola oil

3 cloves garlic, minced

4 tablespoons unsalted butter

1 pound chicken livers, cleaned of any sinew and cut into quarters

2 cups brandy

3 tablespoons all-purpose flour

2½ cups chicken stock, divided

2 or 3 sprigs fresh thyme

2 or 3 sprigs fresh rosemary

For the polenta:

2 cups chicken stock

2 cups whole milk

1 cup polenta

1 cup Fontina cheese, grated

1 teaspoon thyme leaves, finely chopped

Coarse kosher salt and freshly cracked black pepper, to taste

Preheat oven to 375°F. Season the quail on all sides with salt and pepper. Set a large roasting pan across two burners on top of the stove. Turn the heat to medium-high and add canola oil. When the oil is hot, sear the quail until nicely browned on all sides. Remove to a plate and set aside while you make the sauce. (Don't worry, the quail will continue to cook later.)

Reduce the temperature to medium-low. Add minced garlic and butter to the roasting pan and swirl it around until all the yummy brown bits come up from the bottom. Add cleaned livers and cook until lightly browned and coated in pan drippings, about 2–3 minutes. Turn the burners off and add the brandy (you want to do this off the flame, otherwise the alcohol will flare up). Carefully turn the burners back on and bring to a simmer, cooking until the brandy is reduced by half. Sprinkle in flour, whisking to avoid lumps. Whisk in 2 cups chicken stock until all thoroughly combined. Transfer sauce from the roasting pan into a clean sauce pot and let simmer over medium-low heat while you finish the quail, at least 10-15 minutes.

Return the quail to the roasting pan (no need to clean it out). Pour in remaining ½ cup chicken stock and scatter sprigs of thyme and rosemary across the top. Roast in preheated oven until quail is golden brown and cooked through, about 10-15 minutes.

Meanwhile, in a medium pot, combine chicken stock and milk. Gently bring to a simmer taking care not to let the mixture boil or else the milk will separate. Slowly whisk in polenta. Cook over low heat until polenta is tender and all liquid has been absorbed, about 8-10 minutes. Stir in grated cheese and thyme and season with salt and pepper to taste.

When quail is cooked through, remove roasting pan from the oven. Discard the herbs and pour any residual pan juices directly into the gravy pot. Taste gravy and adjust seasoning with salt and pepper. To serve family style, cover the bottom of a deep platter with a layer of polenta. Top with quail and gravy.

THE MACINTOSH

479 King Street, downtown
(843) 789-4299
themacintoshcharleston.com
Executive Chef: Jeremiah Bacon

While it's largely about "the beef" at Oak Steakhouse (see page 166), where Bacon also operates as executive chef, The Macintosh is a more personal baby. After he returned home to Charleston from his laudable stints (including Le Bernadin) in New York City, he felt himself increasingly drawn to serving "approachable fare in a more casual, yet still sleek setting." In conjunction with The Indigo Road Restaurant Group, he created what he calls an "upscale American tavern rooted in Southern, seasonal ingredients."

The Macintosh is rooted in the South, relying on the bounty of the Lowcountry's farms and waterways to inspire unique items with an accessible King Street setting. Dimly lit with a halo-like view into the kitchen where Bacon and his team are almost always visible at work putting out delectable rib-sticking fare like chicken and waffles and a popular Bacon Happy Hour, along with more delicate presentations, such as the stuffed Manchester Quail (see more about Manchester at Cannon Green, page 197) recipe that follows. The Charleston-born chef's dream of devoting his restaurant to the local farmers, fishermen, and purveyors he grew up with came true at The Macintosh, where both his easy going nature and pristine technique driven fare merge to form a truly modern American tavern experience.

Farro verde is an ancient grain from Italy. Like so many smart chefs in Charleston, Bacon buys his wholesale from Anson Mills.

MANCHESTER FARM QUAIL WITH SPRING ONION, ROASTED CHESTNUTS, TURNIPS, AND FARRO VERDE

(SERVES 2–4)

For the glaze:

2 cups sorghum
1 cup sherry vinegar
½ cup fresh lime juice
1 cup soy sauce
1 1-inch length of fresh ginger, peeled
2 cloves garlic
2 shallots
1 tablespoon black peppercorns
½ bunch fresh thyme sprigs

Bring all of the ingredients except the thyme to a boil in a medium pot over high heat. Add the thyme and allow to sit or "steep" for 15–20 minutes. Remove thyme and reduce by half over medium high heat. Set aside. (Note: The glaze can be made ahead and stored in the refrigerator. After that the entire dish comes together very quickly.)

For the chestnut puree:

1 cup chestnuts

1 cup whole cream

4 tablespoons honey

Sea or kosher salt to taste

Preheat oven to 200°F. Arrange the chestnuts on a baking sheet and toast until shells soften. Allow to cool. Remove the flesh from the shells and discard. Puree the chestnuts with the cream and honey until smooth. Season to taste. Reserve warm.

For the farro:

2 tablespoons extra virgin olive oil

1 cup farro verde (a grain from the wheat family)

2½ cups vegetable stock, warm

Sea or kosher salt and freshly ground black pepper to taste

½ cup of reserved turnip greens, cut into fine ribbons (chiffonade)

Heat the olive oil in a medium pot over medium high heat. Add the farro verde and stir to coat. Cook until just toasted and starting to "pop," about 3 minutes. Gradually, stream in the warm stock, in thirds, and stir "risotto style" until the liquid is incrementally absorbed by the farro, about 10 minutes. Season to taste and stir in the turnip greens. Reserve warm.

For the spring onions and turnips:

3 tablespoons unsalted butter

4 spring onions, 2-inches of green stem remaining, halved

4 small spring turnips, scrubbed, peeled, and quartered (reserve greens)

¼ cup water

Sea or kosher salt and freshly ground black pepper to taste

Just before service, melt the butter over medium heat in a medium sauté pan. Add the onions and turnips and season lightly. Cook over medium heat for 5 minutes to get a small amount of color on the vegetables. Add the water (more if needed) and cook until just tender. Reduce off any extra water to a glaze. Season to taste.

For the quail:

2 semi-boneless, 3½ ounce quail (preferably Manchester Farm quail)

½ teaspoon sea or kosher salt

¼ teaspoon freshly ground black pepper

Season the quail on all sides with salt and black pepper. Cook on grill over medium high heat, breast-side down, 3 minutes. Flip to back side and cook another 2 minutes. Remove the quail from the grill and rest 3 minutes.

Plate each quail off-center on a dinner plate over a small bed of warm chestnut puree. Brush each quail generously with the warmed glaze. Top or "stuff" the quail with the farro and artfully scatter the warm onions and turnips on the plate. Serve immediately.

SPECIALTY SHOPS SWEET AND SAVORY

This is an entirely new and equally necessary section to be included in *The New Charleston Chef's Table*. Since the publication of the original in 2009, in addition to so many new incredibly delicious and diverse restaurant and dining options, a series of specialty shops have sprung up from the inventive, entrepreneur-driven minds of Charleston's culinary and oenophile crew.

What every establishment in this section has in common, like the restaurants throughout the book, is excellence, uniqueness, consistency, charm and a wonderfully personalized touch. Also, most were born out of passion. Because the recipes are diverse and in some cases not really applicable to the home cook, I've left them out of this section. But know, if you're in Charleston these specialty shops are absolutely not to be missed.

SWEET SPOTS

Wildflour Pastry

73 Spring Street, downtown, (843) 327-2621
1750 Savannah Highway, West Ashley (843) 990-9391
Wildflourpastrycharleston.com
Chef/Owner: Lauren Mitterer

Lauren Mitterer's external quiet, gentle demeanor and pretty face belie her inner grit and determination. The dual-degreed Culinary Institute of America (Hyde Park) and University of Virginia grad took her respective baking and pastry and studio art degrees, drove down to Charleston and started spinning her magic as executive pastry chef at Red Drum (see page 133). There she developed a formidable name about town (also garnering a James Beard Award nomination) while building a towering customized wedding cake side business.

In 2009, she opened her own pastry shop where she continues to employ an appetizing balance of down home comfort with her flare for artistry and restraint. Citrus Cranberry and Blueberry Lemon sweet scones; buttery, cinnamon smooth and crunchy snickerdoodles; sweet quick breads; assorted muffins; build your own cake (or cupcake)—the options are original and divine. Mitterer draws the largest crowds on Sunday mornings when she serves her warm sticky buns. Lines wrap around the corner at the tiny Spring Street shop. A new location in West Ashley opened this year.

Brown's Court Bakery

199 Saint Philip Street, downtown
(843) 724-0833
Brownscourt.com
Head Baker: David Schnell
Pastry Chef: Carrie Ann Gannon

Another dollhouse of a space with exposed brick, rafters and original flooring, this circa 1800 structure reminds me a lot of Chez Nous (page 150), which is not far away. Schnell and

Gannon combine forces to create bread and pastry creations that are artisanal, delicious, and traditional with an innovative twist.

Sip a mug of steaming hot Counter Culture coffee with a bacon cheddar scone or a knob of chocolate or smoked salt and pepper brioche. The deservedly popular bakery also has a wholesale division which supplies fresh breads to many of the restaurants featured in this book, including Boxcar Betty's (page 91) spongy/soft yet textured fried chicken sandwich bun.

Sugar Bakeshop

59½ Cannon Street, downtown
(843) 579-2891
sugarbake.com
Owners: Bill Bowick and David Bouffard

One of the happiest places I know to go in Charleston, Sugar's taupe and robin's egg blue exterior practically glitters as if it has been sprinkled with the stuff. Inside the tiny, inviting space, Bowick and Bouffard are nearly always visible making their specialized and seasonal cupcakes, pies, tarts, and other "small batch baking" items. The baking team left the hustle and bustle of NYC and architectural careers to open their sugar shop in Charleston in 2007, and the concept was an instant and enduring hit.

The white, soft cake cupcakes generously lathered with caramel buttercream are the stuff of dreams and make the perfect hostess gift or any time there is an occasion to lift your beloved's sweet-tooth spirits. In December, don't miss the opportunity for some of the decadent citrus varieties, especially the orange cupcake made with fresh, local citrus—no extracts here! Lady Baltimore, red velvet, and hummingbird cupcakes are some of the dainty, distinctly southern favorites, but these are made to order only.

Savory Spots

goat.sheep.cow

106 Church Street, downtown, (843) 480-2526
804 Meeting Street, Suite 102, upper peninsula, (843) 203-3118
goatsheepcow.com
Owners: Patty Floersheimer and Trudi Wagner

Two cheese and wine loving friends and smart business women built this business from the ground up and with a fast start in 2011. Correctly billed as a "premier fromagerie," both shops

feature absolutely the best, most nose-blowing selection of cheeses in town, and arguably the Southeast.

Patty and Trudi cull from the finest producers of small production American regional cheese and traditional Euro artisans. The original location on Church Street (South) is housed in a 200 year-old, tiny space with exposed bricks and rafters. It looks and feels just like France and going here is so much fun it will make you smile, no matter how dark your mood. Cured olives, charcuterie, EVO (see EVO page 121) Craft Bakery baguettes, the co-mingling aromas of myriad cheeses, and then, there is wine and mustards and all of that, too. All the fixings for a perfect picnic on The Battery, just a short walk away. Make your own or buy one of GSC's remarkable "daily sandwich" selections (at the South location only). Get there early as they go fast.

Patty and Trudi are almost always in-house and they and their staff are so friendly and accommodating, you feel instantly at home. The ladies opened a larger location (North) on upper Meeting Street in 2016 that boasts a wine and coffee bar where guests can sit down comfortably, chat and nosh on gorgeous cheese between sips of luscious wine.

Bin 152 Wine Bar

152 Queen Street, downtown
(843) 577-7359
bin152.com
Owners: Patrick and Franny Panella

Before they opened Chez Nous (see page 150), this was Patrick and Franny Panella's only business baby. Appropriately nestled in the heart of The French Quarter, it's an ode to Franny's French heritage and the couple's mutual love of cheese and wine. Creamy white bead board walls, polished hardwood floors, and an array of bistro chairs and marble tables give the small space a definite French bistro feel.

There is a corner bar that tends to be populated all through the evenings, largely due to the intimate discourse it avails with either Franny or Patrick as they pick the right wine to pair with one (or more) of their forty cheese choices. Art is hung on the walls for gazing and if sufficiently inspired, purchase. All of the bread is baked fresh daily and the baguettes are crunchy, thin, tubes of Gallic goodness cut to order and lovingly arranged on bread and cheese platters.

Callie's Hot Little Biscuit

476½ King Street, downtown
(843)737-5159
callieshotlittlebiscuit.com
Owner: Carrie Morey

The daughter of beloved Charleston-area caterer Callie White, Carrie Morey deliberately took her mother's locally famous, buttery, diminutive, made-by-hand biscuits viral in 2005 when she founded Callie's Charleston Biscuits. Her intention was to get vast national and online sales and distribution while still keeping her operation small, artisanal, and most importantly, hand-made. She did just that and along the way wrote a cookbook (*Callie's Biscuits and Southern Traditions*) and opened what is, in my opinion, one of the best named little grab-to-go restaurants ever, Callie's Hot Little Biscuit.

Situated on upper King, it's the hot spot for buttery, flaky, hot Southern biscuits, served morning, noon, and night. The kitchen smells of butter, and mint iced tea goes down ever so sweetly. Plain biscuits sandwiched with salty country ham, black pepper bacon biscuits, and cheese and chive are some of the most adored. Unless you count Callie's chunky, sweet/hot pimento cheese sandwiches or even a bowl of grits topped with a fat pat of melting butter.

Rutledge Cab Co.

1300 Rutledge Avenue, upper peninsula
(843) 720-1440
rutledgecabco.com
Executive Chef: Jeff Marshburn

It's breakfast and burgers all day and night at Rutledge Cab Co., a convivial dining and watering hole near the intersection of Rutledge and I-26 on the upper peninsula. But far more than burgers and eggs and hash, RCC (as it's also known) serves a dizzying array of fun, whimsical dishes including Moroccan chicken, kebobs, and a pupu platter served with its very own sterno fire pit.

Executive Chef Jeff Marshburn has been at RCC since it opened in 2014 and relishes putting his personal stamp on the dishes. "For the Reuben, our best-seller, we smoke our own pastrami and cube and chop it. I like fine-tuning our core items and adding little tweaks," explains the Atlanta native and graduate of the last class of Johnson & Wales, Charleston prior to its closing.

Marshburn's chicken and dumplings feature handmade gnocchi, something he mastered while working at an Italian restaurant in Atlanta called Dolce. "I love the comfort of the dish, it's like a meal from Mom feeding three children, but the gnocchi gives it a fluffy, melt-in-your-mouth effect," says Marshburn. There is some prep time involved, about 2 hours, but the results are worth it, and at least the gnocchi and poached chicken and stock can be prepped a day ahead.

Rutledge Cab Co. Chicken and Dumplings

(SERVES 8)

For the potato gnocchi "dumplings":

6 medium russet potatoes, peeled and cut in half

¼ cup sea or kosher salt

Cold water to cover

1 large egg

½ teaspoon freshly grated nutmeg

¼ teaspoon ground black pepper

3 cups all-purpose flour

For the poached chicken:

6 6-ounce boneless chicken breasts

1 quart (4 cups) chicken stock

For the sage gravy:

½ cup unsalted butter, melted

½ cup shallot, minced

1 tablespoon garlic, minced

2 tablespoons fresh thyme leaves, minced

½ cup all-purpose flour

1 quart (4 cups) chicken stock (reserved from poaching chicken)

½ cup heavy cream

¼ cup fresh sage leaves, finely chopped

Sea or kosher salt and freshly ground black pepper to taste

For the buttered bread crumbs:

3 cups panko bread crumbs

2 tablespoons kosher or sea

½ teaspoon ground black pepper

2 tablespoons onion powder

2 tablespoons garlic powder

3 tablespoons fresh parsley leaves, finely chopped

½ cup unsalted butter, melted

For the vegetable mix:

3 tablespoons unsalted butter

2 cups yellow onions, medium dice

1 cup celery, medium dice

1 cup peeled carrots, medium dice

1 cup sweet green peas

1 cup blanched green beans, cut into bite size pieces

¼ cup fresh parsley, finely chopped (for garnish)

Begin with the gnocchi. Cover potatoes with cold water and add salt in a large pot and bring to a slow simmer over medium-low heat. The key to the gnocchi is to cook the potatoes perfectly low and slow. This will generally take about 1 hour. The potato should be just barely fork tender. When done, strain potatoes and immediately pass the warm potatoes through a potato ricer. Let cool in a mixing bowl for 15 minutes. Once cooled add the rest of ingredients except flour, stirring to combine. Add the flour and mix together with a wooden spoon until flour is fully incorporated. Pour the combined dough onto a clean countertop and roll into a thick cylinder. Cut evenly with a knife or a bench scraper into six equal portions. Roll each of the pieces into long, 1-inch thick cylinders (using both hands rolling up and down) until you have an even cylinder. (Note: This needs to be done on a clean un-floured surface. The dough needs to stick to the countertop a little bit or it will slide around.) Once all the dough is rolled out, cover and roll dough in a little flour and line them up evenly. Using bench scraper, cut dough into 1-inch long gnocchi. Place onto a floured cookie sheet and reserve in freezer until ready to use.

Next, poach the chicken. Cover the boneless chicken breasts with the chicken stock in a medium sized pot. Simmer over medium heat for about 20 minutes, or until cooked through. Don't over-cook the chicken or it will fall apart in the gravy. Save the stock and strain it to be used in the gravy. Set the chicken aside. (Refrigerate once cooled unless proceeding immediately with the chicken in the recipe).

For the gravy, start with the shallot, garlic, and thyme, and 1 tablespoon of the melted butter and sweat in a large pot over medium low heat until translucent and tender, about 5 minutes. Add the remaining butter and flour, stir to combine the "roux" and cook for 1 minute over medium-low heat, stirring. Then add chicken stock slowly, whisking the whole time to prevent lumps. Bring to a simmer until thickened, about 5 minutes. Then add the cream and fresh sage. And set aside.

For the buttered bread crumbs, place all the ingredients in the bowl of a food processor fitted with a metal blade, until all are well chopped. Pour the bread crumbs onto a cookie sheet and brown in an oven at 375°F for about 15 minutes, stirring them up half way though for even browning. Set aside.

To finish, bring a large pot of generously salted water to a boil over high. For the vegetable mix, melt the butter in a large sauté pan over medium heat. Add the onion, celery, and carrot and sauté until tender, about 10 minutes. Meanwhile, cut the poached chicken into bite-sized pieces and add to the sauté pan with the vegetables. Add gravy base and bring back to a slow simmer over medium heat. Add the peas and green beans. Then add gnocchi to the slow boiling water (you don't want rapid boiling water because dumplings will fall apart) and cook for about 3-5 minutes (or until they float and add 1 more minute). Pull gnocchi from water with a slotted spoon and add to gravy. Taste and season with more salt and pepper if needed. Garnish with fresh parsley. Serve warm in bowls topped with buttered bread crumbs.

Just Desserts

Maybe they're all on a sugar high or have visions of sugarplums dancing in their happy heads, but the chefs featured in this sweet chapter are surely a contented and whimsical lot. Their joy shows up in their smiles and their confections.

At 181 Palmer, admired chef and instructor Scott Stefanelli composes a Reese's-like blend of peanut butter and chocolate mousse served on a chocolate-coconut cookie crisp. See Wee's old-fashioned, homespun appeal delights in a thick coconut cake dressed with a fluffy seven-minute frosting honed to perfection. Nobody's pastry fool, Cynthia Wong whips magic from buttermilk in her creamy, pink, sweet tart buttermilk rhubarb fool, while Pawpaw's Davee Harned hits a Southern, soulful homerun with butterscotch pudding and molasses ginger cookies. Banana bread gets a brush of burnt caramel love from The Granary's Brannon Florie for an extra sweet and crunchy finish.

181 Palmer

Culinary Institute of Charleston/Trident Technical College—Palmer Campus
66 Columbus Street, downtown
For reservations (required): (843) 820-5087, ext. 2
culinaryinstituteofcharleston.com
Chef: Scott Stefanelli and students

If it weren't situated on a campus and if the servers and cooks weren't so young, you'd swear you were at a five-star restaurant. In fact, you are in a live culinary classroom at 181 Palmer, where the advanced-level hospitality and culinary students work the stations of a real restaurant to prepare for real-life work. It sounds serious, but these kids have a ball. The servers, clad in black and with notepads in hand, exude joy and enthusiasm. It comes through in the food, too. Beautifully presented and impeccable, it's proof that this kitchen is 100 percent on.

Veteran chef and long-term instructor Scott Stefanelli is at the center of it all. This living laboratory gives him an opportunity to do what he loves most—teach. "I like being a chef and teaching for the same reason. Both jobs give me a chance to mentor," he says. Scott creates a new menu for each semester—spring, fall, and summer—that revolves around seasonal produce and core techniques he aims to teach.

Reservations are required, either by phone or online, and 181 Palmer closes for a brief time between semesters. Visit the site for schedule and menu updates.

This Reese's-Cup-on-culinary-steroids recipe employs two different mousse-making techniques and features an engaging interplay between cool and crunchy. The bananas are a warm garnish and are prepared just before serving.

PEANUT BUTTER AND MILK CHOCOLATE MOUSSE WITH COCONUT CRUNCH AND CARAMELIZED BANANAS

(SERVES 12)

For the coconut crunch:

¾ cup heavy cream

1½ cups dark chocolate, finely chopped

1 cup flaked coconut, toasted until lightly brown

½ cup hazelnuts, finely chopped and toasted

2 cups crumbled French waffle cookies or Piroulines

For the chocolate mousse:

2 cups small pieces milk chocolate

½ stick (4 tablespoons) unsalted butter

3 eggs, separated

1 tablespoon water

¼ cup granulated sugar

1 teaspoon vanilla extract

1½ cups heavy cream

For the peanut butter mousse:

2 cups heavy cream

3 gelatin sheets or 1½ teaspoons powdered gelatin

4 eggs

½ cup powdered sugar

1½ cups good-quality peanut butter

For the caramelized bananas:

4 large bananas, peeled and sliced into rounds

Juice of ½ lemon

¼ cup dark rum

½ stick (4 tablespoons) unsalted butter

¼ cup brown sugar

First, prepare the coconut crunch. Spray an 11-inch springform pan lightly with a cooking spray. In a medium, heavy-bottomed pan, heat the cream over high heat until it comes to a boil. Put the chocolate in a medium bowl and pour the hot cream over it. Stir until the chocolate has melted completely. Fold in the remaining ingredients and mix just until the chocolate has coated everything. Press the mixture into the bottom of the springform pan and spread evenly. Refrigerate until ready to fill with the mousse.

To make the chocolate mousse, put the chocolate and butter in a large bowl and place over a gently simmering water bath. Melt gently and slowly, stirring. Remove from the heat to cool slightly, but do not allow the ganache to harden. Meanwhile, combine the egg yolks, water, sugar, and vanilla in a medium bowl over the same simmering water bath and whisk vigorously until thick ribbons form, about 4 minutes. Fold this mixture into the ganache. In a medium bowl, whip the egg whites with a hand-held blender or whisk until soft peaks form. Fold the egg whites into the chocolate mixture. (Scott says, "the mixture may seem grainy at this point, but fear not, it will come together.") In a medium bowl, whip the cream with a handheld blender or whisk until peaks form. Gently fold the whipped cream into the chocolate mixture, then gently transfer the mixture to the prepared springform. Tap the pan lightly on the counter until the mousse is level. Cover with plastic and refrigerate for at least 2 hours before proceeding.

To prepare the peanut butter mousse, heat 1 cup of the cream in a small pot over medium-high heat to bring to a simmer. Remove from the heat and add the gelatin. Whisk gently to dissolve. Set aside, keeping warm enough to prevent the gelatin from setting. In a medium bowl over a simmering water bath, vigorously whisk together the eggs and powdered sugar until thickened. (The mixture should form thick ribbons and have the smooth, liquid pudding weight of a sabayon sauce.) Cool immediately by placing the bowl over a larger bowl filled with ice water. Stir to facilitate the cooling process.

Whip the remaining 1 cup of cream in a medium bowl with a handheld blender or whisk until soft peaks form. Place the peanut butter in the bowl of a mixer fitted with the paddle attachment. Turn the mixer on at low speed and gradually add the cream and gelatin mixture until completely incorporated. Scrape the sides of the bowl with a spatula to make sure the peanut butter is fully incorporated. Remove the paddle, scraping off any excess peanut butter mixture and returning it to the bowl. Fold in the warm egg and sugar mixture by hand. With a spatula, gently stir in ⅓ of the whipped cream. Fold in the remaining cream, gently, in two parts. The mousse should have a smooth, fluffy consistency. Spoon the peanut butter mousse on top of the chocolate mousse in the springform pan. Spread evenly and tap the pan to level it. Refrigerate, covered with plastic, for at least 4 hours, but preferably overnight. (The mousse can also be frozen in the springform pan for several days and thawed in the refrigerator before serving.)

Just before serving, prepare the bananas. Toss the banana slices with lemon juice and rum in a medium bowl. Set aside. Heat a medium sauté pan over medium heat. Add butter and sugar and cook until the sugar is dissolved and the mixture begins to bubble. Add the bananas and heat through, about 5 minutes.

To serve, gently unmold the mousse and slice into wedges as you might a cheesecake. Serve a wedge on each plate with a few slices of warm bananas and their sauce alongside.

See Wee Restaurant

4808 Highway 17 North, Awendaw
(843) 928-3609
seeweerestaurant.com
Owner: Mary Rancourt

Before it became a restaurant, this roadside bungalow was a general store known as See Wee Supply. About thirty miles north of downtown, it's neatly nestled between the sprawl of Mount Pleasant and the fishing village charm of McClellanville, a little farther up the road. It has drawn hungry travelers and lovers of hush puppies, fried seafood, and killer cakes for nearly twenty years, happily with no signs of stopping or slowing down its steady stream of good eats and rural allure.

True to her plan, Rancourt kept all the general store kitsch when she transformed the store into a restaurant and culled a mix of family recipes (what she calls "good home cooking") to create the simple-yet-satisfying menu. Her sister, Amy White, and sister-in-law help with baking the cakes and pies for which See Wee is known. See Wee's Old-Fashioned Coconut Cake is Amy's baby and, accordingly, she speaks of it with love. "It's something that's evolved through trial and error. I finally got it to just where I wanted it. It's the soft seven-minute frosting that makes it so good," says Amy.

A dandy of a cake, it's not too sweet, it's full of moisture, and it's See Wee's longstanding best-selling dessert.

SEE WEE'S OLD-FASHIONED COCONUT CAKE

(SERVES 8)

For the cake:

1 stick (¼ pound) unsalted butter

1½ cups granulated sugar

2 eggs, plus 2 egg yolks (reserve the whites for the frosting)

2 cups self-rising flour (White Lily)

1 cup milk

1 teaspoon vanilla extract

For the frosting:

1½ cups granulated sugar

1 teaspoon cream of tartar

Dash of salt

2 egg whites

⅓ cup water

½ teaspoon coconut extract

For the garnish:

2 cups dried coconut flakes

Preheat the oven to 350°F and bring all the cake ingredients to room temperature. Cream together the butter and sugar in a large bowl with a hand mixer at medium speed, until frothy and light. Add the egg yolks and beat for 2 minutes to combine. Add the whole eggs and repeat. Turn the mixer to its slowest speed and slowly add the flour and milk to the batter, alternating ¼-cup quantities of each. Finally, blend in the vanilla.

Grease and flour two 9-inch cake pans and pour the batter into them, tapping to level the cakes. Bake for 25 minutes or until the cake springs back to the touch. Remove from the oven and cool for a few minutes. Run a flat spatula around the edges of the pans to loosen the cakes. Turn them out onto cooling racks and allow to cool completely before frosting.

To make the 7-minute frosting, prepare a boiling water bath over high heat in a large pot. Combine all ingredients except the coconut extract in a medium heat-proof bowl and beat with a hand mixer on high speed over the warm water for exactly 7 minutes—hence the name. Be sure not to let the bowl touch the boiling water; it should sit just above it. Amy says the frosting will be "very fluffy and stand in peaks." Remove frosting from the heat and fold in the coconut extract.

To prepare the coconut for the cake, place it in a food processor fitted with a steel blade and pulse 3 to 5 times. Amy insists this makes the cake easier to slice and serve.

To frost the cake, working on a cake stand, frost the top of the bottom layer of the cake generously and sprinkle generously with the coconut. Top with the second cake layer, frost the top generously, and sprinkle generously with the coconut. Frost the sides of the cake and, cupping the coconut in the palm of your hands, press the coconut into the sides.

From here, slice, serve, and eat!

PawPaw

209 East Bay Street, downtown
(843) 297-4443
pawpawrestaurant.com
Pastry Chef: DaVee Harned

In addition to being ridiculously fun to say, pawpaw is a short season fruit grown throughout the South. Unlike a persimmon, it's a relatively rare find that many (including myself and Pawpaw's pastry chef DaVee Harned) have not had the opportunity to sample, though she's heard it described as a cross between a mango and a banana.

Harned's "fun and Southern" creations are as much as possible inspired by the season from the key lime pie right down to the last, delicious crumb of her coconut cake. Though young, she's worked in several notable Charleston kitchens and holds a Johnson & Wales (Charlotte) degree in baking and pastry arts, but it was her time in Florence and Sicily, Italy that left a permanent mark on her culinary career. "It seems like it lasted forever, yet it went so quickly," she laments.

She's a sentimental cook, too. "My favorite things to make when I was little were frosted cut-out cookies with my grandmother. I knew then that I wanted to work doing something I actually enjoy doing. I cannot imagine doing anything else."

Her silky butterscotch pudding, with a nutty, caramel aroma and flavor is the perfect foil to her chewy, crunchy molasses ginger cookies, which are her favorite component of the entire dish. "Mom used to make them every year for Christmas. Sometimes, when I can't go home for Christmas, I make them for myself. It's almost like going home." Top off your cooled custard with a fat dollop of whipped cream and a cookie on the side.

Butterscotch Pudding

(SERVES 6–8)

4 tablespoons unsalted butter

2 teaspoons vanilla bean paste (or substitute pure vanilla extract)

¾ cup dark brown sugar

2 cups heavy cream

1½ cups whole milk

7 egg yolks

¼ cup cornstarch

¼ cup granulated sugar

1 tablespoon bourbon (optional)

½ teaspoon sea or kosher salt

Over medium heat melt the butter. Cook until the butter begins to brown and have a nutty aroma. Add the vanilla and the brown sugar. Cook for a few minutes. The sugar will start to dissolve and come to a light simmer. While whisking, slowly add the cream and milk. Once the cream and milk are incorporated bring mixture back to a simmer over medium heat to dissolve any sugar clumps that might have formed.

Separately, whisk the yolks and cornstarch together in a medium bowl until smooth. While whisking, slowly stream in the hot cream mixture into the yolk mixture and add the bourbon and salt. Return the mixture to the cooking pot and cook over medium heat, whisking, until thickened and the starchy taste is gone—about 5 minutes. Run the mixture through a fine strainer into the bowl of a mixer. Stir the mixture on low speed with a paddle attachment. This will allow the pudding to cool and not overcook.

Portion the pudding into desired serving dishes. Cover directly with plastic wrap until ready to serve to prevent a skin from forming. Let the pudding set completely in the fridge for a few hours before serving.

MOLASSES GINGER COOKIES

(MAKES ABOUT 2 DOZEN COOKIES)

¾ cup shortening
1 cup granulated sugar
¼ cup molasses
1 whole egg
2¼ cups all-purpose flour
2 teaspoons ground ginger
1 teaspoon baking soda
1 teaspoon ground cinnamon
¾ teaspoon ground cloves
Pinch sea or kosher salt
½ cup extra granulated sugar, for coating

Preheat oven to 325°F. In a large bowl, cream or whisk together the shortening, sugar, and molasses. Add the egg, combining, and scraping down the bowl as needed. Separately, in a medium bowl, whisk together the flour, ginger, baking soda, cinnamon, cloves, and salt. Add the dry ingredients to the shortening and molasses mixture in thirds, stirring with a wooden spoon to combine.

Use a small ice cream scoop to form each cookie and roll both through a small bowl of the ½ cup sugar coating. Place the cookie dough on to a baking pan leaving enough space between each cookie to allow for spreading. Bake for 10 minutes rotating the pan halfway through. Cool on cooling racks. (Note: The cookies can be made a day or two ahead, cooled, and stored in an air-sealed container.)

CHANTILLY (WHIPPED CREAM)

(MAKES ABOUT 2 CUPS)

¾ cup heavy cream, cold
1 tablespoon powdered sugar
½ teaspoon vanilla extract

Whip all ingredients together to a medium-stiff peak

To serve, place a generous dollop of Chantilly on each chilled pudding and "pierce" each pudding with a cookie.

THE DAILY (BY BUTCHER & BEE)

652 King Street, upper peninsula
(843) 619-0151
shopthedaily.com

Executive Pastry Chef Butcher & Bee and The Daily: Cynthia Wong

"It smells like morning," says four-time nominated James Beard Outstanding Pastry Chef, Cynthia Wong, of her "daily" office where her days usually begin at 4 a.m. "It's a lovely space, lovely location, and a crowd there that already loves it," Wong beams. Her plate is full of responsibilities to keep them that way. She oversees a large wholesale bread business (for Butcher & Bee) as well as pastries for The Daily. The menu is vast and glorious including breads, breakfast pastries, ice cream sandwiches, sorbets, and what Wong calls "the whole spectrum."

One thousand croissants come out of her temperature-controlled prep room a week, and another 300–400 pastries a day. "I always knew I wanted to be a baker or a pastry chef ever since I was little, so I did it," in a big, big way. Wong split her childhood between Nashville and Mobile, Alabama and continues to be inspired by the Southern seasons. "I love fruit, maybe even better than chocolate, but I like that a lot."

The early-spring inspired buttermilk rhubarb fool was something Wong created for another "gig" prior to The Daily. "I wanted something small, fresh, with a sweet bite and very balanced all the way through," she says of this light, fruity creamy dish that is just as lovely to look at as it is to eat.

BUTTERMILK RHUBARB FOOL

(SERVES 6–8)

For the rhubarb:

4 cups fresh rhubarb, sliced into ½-inch chunks

2 cups water

2 cups granulated sugar

1 vanilla bean

For the fool:

1¾ cups heavy cream

1-2 tablespoons sugar

½ cup buttermilk

Wash the rhubarb and slice into ½-inch chunks. Make a vanilla syrup by placing the sugar and water in a medium pot. Cut the vanilla bean in half crosswise, and scrape out the seeds. Place the bean and seeds in the pot with the sugar and vanilla and cook over medium-high heat.

When the syrup comes to a rolling boil, add the rhubarb to the pot. Let the syrup come back to a boil, then take the pot off the stove and pour the syrup and rhubarb into a heat-proof container. Let the rhubarb cool to room temperature. Reserve 1 cup of the poached rhubarb pieces. Puree the rest in a blender. Add more sugar, or lemon juice, as needed to correct the flavor.

You can use the rhubarb puree as is, or you can take an extra step, which is what Chef Wong does at Pawpaw. Churn the puree in an ice cream maker until it is frozen. Scrape the frozen mixture out of the machine and into a container, then let it "thaw." Chef Wong uses it when it's half-frozen, so that it is very cold and very airy and light—no longer a sorbet, but lighter and colder than a sauce.

To prepare the "fool," whip the heavy cream with just enough sugar to lightly sweeten. When it's close to soft peaks but not fully there yet, add the buttermilk and rewhip. It won't be as thick as whipped cream, but it will definitely be airy and light.

To serve, layer fool and rhubarb puree in alternating layers in chilled glasses. Top with the pieces of poached rhubarb. Serve immediately.

The Granary

835 Coleman Boulevard, Mount Pleasant
(843) 216-3832
thegranarycharleston.com
Executive Chef/Partner: Brannon Florie

For equal part entrepreneur and chef Brannon Florie, being a chef wasn't always part of the plan. "I went into it backwards. I started my first business, a landscaping outfit, when I was 12. I always wanted to own something, some kind of business, but then I realized I was a good cook," explains Florie. It wasn't until after he worked with some "really great chefs" from all over the world at Disney, that Florie got really serious about cooking.

He's had his hand in myriad cooking business pots locally and elsewhere including restaurant consulting, menu development, and developing a serious passion for charcuterie. At The Granary, a term for a grain house or silo, Florie likes to make food that's "approachable, and recognizable with lots of variety and seasonal changes." He calls his food, "for the people!" And, case in point, who doesn't love banana bread? His gets a nice caramel crunch and a creamy caramel ice cream touch. "It's good, just simple and easy to do at home. I think I have made it better and better over the years."

BANANA BREAD BRÛLÉE WITH CARAMEL ICE CREAM

(SERVES 8)

1 stick (½ cup) unsalted butter, room temperature

5 ripe bananas

1 cup granulated sugar

1 egg

⅛ teaspoon sea or kosher salt

1½ teaspoons vanilla extract

½ teaspoons baking powder

2 cups all-purpose flour

½ cup light brown sugar, to caramelize

Caramel vanilla ice-cream (or favorite vanilla or other complementary flavor)

¼ cup toasted pistachios, for garnish

Preheat oven to 350°F. In a stand mixer, mix butter, banana, sugar, egg, salt, and vanilla on low until incorporated. Slowly add sifted flour and baking powder. Do not over mix. This also can be done with a hand mixer or just by hand. Butter a 1# loaf pan, pour banana batter into loaf pan, and cover with foil. Cook covered for 45 minutes. Take foil off and cook another 15 minutes uncovered or until brown.

Once cooled, slice ½-inch or desired thickness. Spread 1 tablespoon of light brown sugar over one side of the bread. Put back in oven for 2–3 minutes until warm. With a small kitchen crème brûlée torch, lightly torch brown sugar until it caramelizes. (Note: You can also crème brûlée the sugar under a broiler heated on high. Watch closely!) Add 1 scoop of your favorite ice cream and drizzle generously with toasted pistachios.

INDEX

ABOUT THE AUTHOR

Holly Herrick is a former restaurant critic and features writer at Charleston's daily newspaper, *The Post and Courier*. She is a classically trained chef with a Grande Diplome from Le Cordon Bleu Paris and a graduate of Boston College. A first-place nationally awarded food writer by the Association of Food Journalists, she is the author of eight cookbooks and has contributed articles to *Southern Living, Gourmet, Food & Wine, Charleston Style and Design,* and several Southern regional publications. She lives in Charleston with her tuxedo cat, Mr. Purrfect and choclate cocker spaniel Rocky. For more information or to contact Holly, visit hollyherrick.com.